MW01613837

EMPOWERING Long-Term ELs

with Social Emotional Learning, Language and Literacy

Margarita Calderón   Hector Montenegro

Praise for EMPOWERING LONG-TERM ELS WITH SOCIAL EMOTIONAL LEARNING, LANGUAGE, AND LITERACY:

"The trauma and stress invoked by multiple crises in recent history have been the platform for bringing social-emotional learning to the forefront of educators' attention. Calderón and Montenegro have skillfully taken the leap into the world of English learners and have applied principles of SEL to the unique circumstances and issues facing LTELs. The authors should be applauded for seamlessly integrating high expectations and rigorous instructional practices into SEL teaching so that these middle and high schoolers have every opportunity to succeed."

-Margo Gottlieb, *Ph.D., WIDA co-founder and lead developer, Wisconsin Center for Education Research, University of Wisconsin-Madison; former Director of Assessment and Evaluation, Illinois Resource Center; author/co-author of over 20 books*

"*EMPOWERING LONG-TERM ELs* is filling a huge gap in the field of Social and Emotional Learning--this is the book we've all been waiting for! Calderon and Montenegro have done a masterful job crafting an invaluable resource for all educators and educational leaders committed to championing SEL in service of equity."

- Meena Srinivasan, *Executive Director, Transformative Educational Leadership, Author of SEL Every Day: Integrating Social and Emotional Learning with Instruction in Secondary Classrooms & Teach, Breathe, Learn: Mindfulness In and Out of the Classroom*

"There are many books that are focused on social emotional learning, language, or literacy. *EMPOWERING LONG-TERM ELs* delineates the important connection among these topics. This book provides a roadmap for education as a key tool for transformative systemic change if justice is going to be a reality. Voices from educators in the field, instructional strategies, and protocols for adult learning through collaboration are details outlined in the roadmap."

- Janice E. Jackson, *EdD, Senior Advisor Equity and Inclusion for Transformative Educational Leadership; former Deputy Superintendent for Boston Public Schools, former Deputy Assistant Secretary for the Office of Secretary Education for the US Depart of Education*

Copyright © 2021 Montenegro Consulting Group, LLC and Margarita Calderón
Published by Velázquez Press,
A division of Academic Learning Company, LLC

Cover Photo Copyright © Dr. Hector Montenegro

No part of this work may be reproduced or transmitted in any form or by any means, electronic or mechanical, including photocopying and recording, or by an information storage or retrieval system without the prior written permission of Velázquez Press, unless such copying is expressly permitted by federal copyright law. All inquiries should be addressed to:

Velázquez Press 9682 Telstar Ave., Ste. 110
El Monte, CA 91731 USA

www.VelazquezPress.com

ISBN 10: 1-59495-771-1
ISBN 13: 978-1-59495-771-0 (Paperback)

ISBN 10: 1-59495-793-2
ISBN 13: 978-1-59495-793-2 (EBook + Video)

Printed in the United States

First Edition

25 24 23 22 21 1 2 3 4 5

Library of Congress Control Number: 2021932169

4

Table of CONTENTS

Acknowledgments

irst, we would like to offer our heartfelt thanks to Arthur Chou for recognizing the importance of the topic for this book; David Olvera and Lui Vega, our editors, who made it flow; and Jonathan Ruiz, who kept reminding us of the end goal.

Additionally, we would like to thank all the English as a second language (ESL) and core content teachers, instructional coaches, principals, other site administrators, and district administrators who have worked with us these past few years. Their commitment to English learners (Els) has been amazing and rarely recognized as it should be. You know who you are, and we applaud you and look forward to continuing this journey with you. By the same token we want to thank the dedicated Department of Education leaders from Virginia, North Carolina who sponsored our professional development and institutes throughout the years.

Finally, Margarita and Hector owe special thanks to those who subsidized this collaborative framework. For Margarita: there have been many grants that underwrote my research, but I would like to thank Bob Slavin and Johns Hopkins University for supporting all my work. I want to continue to thank Andrés Henríquez and the Carnegie Corporation of New York for funding the Expediting Comprehension for English Language Learners/Accelerando la Comprensión en Español (ExC-ELL™/ ACE-LERA™) models that continue to create success for multilingual learners all over the world.

For Hector: words cannot express my appreciation for the Collaborative for Academic, Social, and Emotional Learning (CASEL) for leading the way in making social and emotional learning (SEL) a priority for classrooms, districts, states, and the nation. I am most grateful to all of the dedicated and committed staff at CASEL who have taken SEL to a new level by making resources, guides, and research available for access globally. Many thanks to Ann McKay Bryson, CASEL consultant, for your support in the research and editing of this manuscript. I am especially grateful to the original CASEL consultants who paved the way and set the bar high for school districts to implement SEL systemically. It has been a labor of love and of tremendous learning. I especially want to acknowledge Sue Keister, my CASEL colleague for six years with the Sacramento City Unified School District (SCUSD), from whom I learned most about SEL implementation and mindfulness. I must also recognize the leadership team of Transformative Educational Leadership (TEL), Meena Srinivasan, Linda Lanteri, Janice Jackson, Daniel Rechtschaffen, and Kristine Mathiasen, who are leading the way for educational leaders at all levels to integrate equity, SEL, mindfulness, and leadership at an inner personal level in order to create outer systemic transformation. I am honored to serve on the TEL board and as a faculty member. ■

Dedication

For my parents, grandparents, aunts, and uncles who dedicated their lives as teachers, principals, and professors to educating so many in Mexico and who set the example for me, my brother and sister, and my son.

Margarita Calderón

Dedicated to my mother and father, Jose and Zita, who worked hard, sacrificed much, and made it possible for their five boys to be successful and to my family, Raquel, Fabiana, and Celina, for your support, patience, and love.

Hector Montenegro

Foreword

inally, a book on social and emotional learning (SEL) for Long-Term English learners (LTELs). This book will help educators provide English learners (ELs) with an equal opportunity in their academic pursuits without feeling ashamed or embarrassed by their developing English language skills. More importantly, this book serves as a guide for those educators who need an easy and quick reference on steps to take to achieve the ultimate goal—to offer *every* child a fair and equitable education, LTELs in particular.

As a superintendent of schools, I know the road of an EL well because I traveled this road as a student. I was born in Puerto Rico and moved to Wisconsin as a teenager. Since my first language is Spanish, I had difficulty speaking English, but I was not alone as many of my friends had the same experience. To make things worse, many teachers were unable to understand or recognize our dilemma because, in their defense, they were not adequately trained to, nor expected to, teach us any differently from our English native-speaking peers.

Like Sandra's story in chapter one, we were often ridiculed, bullied, and treated as inferior. Consequently, we were afraid to speak up in class for fear of being called stupid. Being taught English using the pre-kinder and kindergarten curriculum did not work for the older children. More than a few of my friends never made it out of the English as a second language classes and eventually became discouraged and fell through the proverbial crack, as a result, so many never graduated.

We did not dare go home to tell our parents how we were ridiculed and neglected socially, emotionally and academically because our parents, like in most Latino households, thought so highly of teachers and expected us to behave, show respect, and not complain. Because of the language barrier, our parents were not connected to the schools, and the schools rarely reached out to them, and if they did, it was not in Spanish. Throughout my years in school we were labeled as "Los Tontos" by our peers with English proficiency. I learned to reject rejection early in life through the strong foundation instilled in me by my grandparents and mother, coupled with a support system from my siblings and newcomer students who experienced the same struggles.

Because of my experience as an EL, I challenged and applied myself in school and persevered. I became a teacher to help students who, like me, struggled with learning English as quickly as expected. Through my experience, I learned that teachers who are inclusive and showed compassion, empathy, and respect while having high academic standards are more likely to engage their EL students academically, therefore eliminating the chance that they would become Long-Term ELs. However, even after grasping the language, I was still labeled a non-native English speaker, primarily because of my accent. Today, I still have a slight accent, but I also have a Ph.D. and I am very proud of both!

I was fortunate to have a number of teachers and mentors along the way who helped me pursue my dream of helping *all* students. One of my mentors is a co-author of this book, Dr. Hector Montenegro. I have known Dr. Montenegro since I was a principal in Wisconsin. He helped guide me through some of my most difficult challenges as an educator and always made himself available. During my first superintendency in Illinois, he often came to my district to share his knowledge and expertise on Social and Emotional Learning (SEL) with my faculty and staff. After working with Dr. Montenegro, my team always wanted him back for professional development days. At the time, he was working with the Collaborative for Academic, Social, and Emotional Learning (CASEL), and SEL was being implemented in districts throughout the country. He is proficient in his knowledge and understanding of this practice. This book, developed in collaboration with Dr. Margarita Calderón, a pioneer and researcher in English Language Learning, is one you will refer to again and again on how to support English learners' academic and social and emotional development effectively.

I am proud to recommend this book to all my colleagues in education and to parents who want a better understanding of how social and emotional learning is desperately needed in schools and every classroom, especially for those classrooms that serve LTELs. We need to do more to prevent and eliminate the pipeline from an EL to an LTEL. The integration of SEL should be implemented systematically and effectively into language and literacy at all levels. The inquiry in this book is intentional, as it seeks to provide an understanding of the experiences, challenges, and opportunities confronting ELs in their attempt to define and establish themselves in American schools.

The book provides a framework for schools to get started integrating SEL and literacy strategies into the curriculum. It outlines how these strategies can support the instructional practices that may already be in place to support ELs. With the proper support and care, ELs can and will transition into the academic, linguistic, and cultural mainstream rather than becoming LTELs. As stated in this book, I strongly agree that the "plight of LTELs is not clearly understood, largely ignored, and attempts at prevention and intervention have been poorly designed and inconsistently implemented." For this reason, I consider this book by two experienced and gifted authors and educators an essential resource in launching the effort to systemically and systematically eliminate the "gap" that should never exist in the first place.

Respectfully,
Dr. Jesse J. Rodriguez
Superintendent
Zion-Benton Township High School District 126, Zion, IL

Introduction
SEL and LTELs

*t*he plight of Long-Term English learners (LTELs) is of concern to educators, parents, researchers, and community leaders. There are many success stories about ELs beating the odds by graduating and continuing their education and becoming contributing members of their community. On the other hand, it is anticipated that the numbers of LTELs nationwide will continue to increase due to the added challenges of the pandemic and its impact on the economy, education, and health. What many are calling the COVID Slide, the loss of academic gain due to the inconsistent and broken patterns of formal education throughout the country, will most negatively impact ELs and LTELs who lack financial resources and academic support (Olsen 2010).

As a result of the switch to distance, hybrid learning or even gradual returning to class, teachers are now being required to modify their curriculum, pedagogy, and ability to create a climate and culture that is more inclusive and nurturing. Compounding the consequences of social distancing is the communication gap between English-dominant students and ELs. Educators overall and their students would greatly benefit from learning and practicing the basic skills and competencies of social and emotional learning (SEL) to better address the consequences of the current social isolation.

LTELs need more opportunities to interact with English-dominant students. For an LTEL to be able to practice English and learn current cultural norms from native English speakers is considered one of the greatest motivating factors for ELs and LTELs to want to learn the language and participate in mainstream classes and activities. Teachers who place a high premium on actively building an inclusive, interactive, and engaging learning environment where ELs learn from English-speaking peers, results in the further development of SEL competencies of having empathy and compassion for others, valuing diversity, appreciating other cultures, and possessing relationship skills for English-dominant students.

Families who are better resourced financially are able to provide their children with an abundance of food and secure housing, guaranteed Internet connectivity, computer equipment, exposure to learning materials, and resources comparable to home schooling practitioners. On the other hand, ELs who live in poverty, whose parents are experiencing job, food, medical, and housing insecurity, are often forced to live in overcrowded conditions, making social distancing and quarantine practices nearly impossible. Many older LTELs are having to look for jobs to help to support the family, which pushes them further behind the learning curve. With this added stress, uncertainty, and even emotional trauma, the focus on academic learning and English language acquisition for many ELs is secondary to basic survival needs.

We know that adolescents in general are struggling with the surge of hormones, self-identity crisis, and social pressures to belong and to be accepted. Left emotionally unregulated, teens run the risk of making unwise decisions and engaging in dangerous and socially unacceptable behavior in addition to experiencing higher rates of stress and depression. According to a pre-pandemic Pew Research Center survey, 70 percent of teens say anxiety and depression is a "major problem" among their peers, making anxiety the mental health tsunami of their generation (Flannery 2019). If the same survey were administered in late 2020, we can safely assume that the percentages would be significantly higher.

Nationally, as students are gradually returning to the classroom, initial indicators are that the achievement gap has widened exponentially. Exclusive focus on academic achievement and high stakes testing is not what students need at this time, nor in the near future. Adapting to this new normal of social separation and the return to a completely altered learning environment is putting tremendous pressure on educators to modify their styles of teaching, leading, and interacting. Adults not only need to attend to their own emotional well-being and health care but have to be more sensitive to the emotional trauma and academic decline of their most vulnerable students, especially their ELs.

The purpose of this book is to offer strategies, resources, and information that would support the integration of language, literacy, and SEL into core subject areas taught in the K–12 schools. Albeit many examples in this book are for secondary grades due to the urgency to further prevent inequities for LTELs. This schooling hiatus and upheaval is actually a great opportunity to reconstruct what has not worked so far. This is the time to think deeply and become relentless in the pursuit of better instructional delivery, whether remote or in-person or blended.

In chapter one, we use a real-life story of an LTEL (names have been changed to protect identities) to set the stage for schools and districts to be hyper-vigilant in safeguarding against such a scenario occurring in schools. The research on social and emotional learning and a sample of instructional practices are laid out in this chapter.

In chapter two, we elaborate on the need to integrate language, literacy, and content with SEL competencies as essential for all students and especially for LTELs. We ourselves need SEL to manage our own well-being while keeping in mind that LTEL need us more now than ever. This chapter reminds us of what has not worked in the past as we move forward to remedy injustices and misconceptions. This chapter suggests ways to teach in a new educational setting and makes suggestions as to how to make use of new instructional tools such as online bulletin boards, virtual whiteboards, and shared online documents.

Chapter three explores platforms to enhance SEL, language, and blended Instruction by taking a deeper look at the Three Signature Practices of SEL, incorporating the framework of Welcoming Routines and Rituals, Engaging Pedagogy and Strategies and Optimistic Closures as the guiding outline for the chapter.

Chapter four elaborates on the need to teach the academic language by integrating SEL standards and strategies that LTELs, and many other students, would greatly benefit from. When teachers begin using the vocabulary strategies as described in this chapter, they discover that they are just as beneficial for all students, not just LTELs.

Chapter five goes into detail on how to teach reading in a way that creates enthusiasm for reading in an SEL context. This includes illustrating several ways to practice close reading for information processing and mastery while helping students strengthen their SEL competencies, such as developing positive relationships and showing empathy for their peers. The abundance of SEL skills that are developed through cooperative reading are highlighted and ways to set up well-functioning partnerships and teams are described.

Chapter six builds upon the reading that students are doing and connects it with specific writing assignments. Once again, focusing on further developing SEL competencies and skills while working in teams becomes the key for integrating academic vocabulary, discourse, reading comprehension, content mastery, and writing skills. Academic and workplace writing calls for different genres, different audiences, different purposes, and different approaches.

Chapter seven is intended to tie it all together. Reflections in this chapter will help achieve a clear picture of this book and applications that will benefit LTELs.

A note on visuals: unless cited otherwise, all graphs and charts are original works of the authors created for this book.

We hope you find this book informative, practical, and, ultimately, transformative. ■

Chapter 1
Why SEL for LTELs

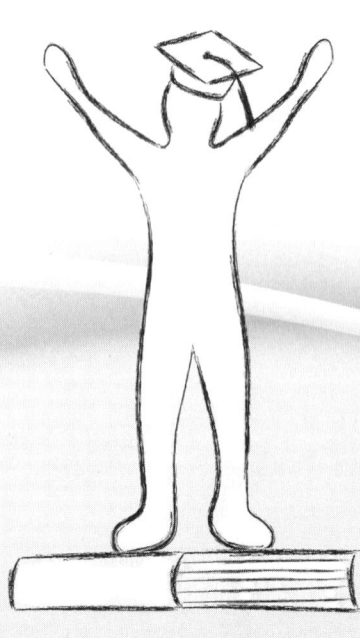

a s a six-year-old moving to this country from Mexico, the first thing Sandra's parents did was to enroll her in a public school. The school placed her into English as a second language (ESL) classes and for the first four years of school she became fluent in English. "By second grade my English was basically 'perfect' compared to your average American student."

Sandra used to love ESL classes in elementary school but once she got to middle school, "I was pulled out of class to 'learn' a language that I already knew." The ESL classes were taught at a very slow pace, and the teachers leading the classes barely spoke English themselves. "When I was in sixth grade, they just taught basic things like colors and animals at a first grade level. What I was learning in my ESL classes was not relevant or supportive of my regular classes. It was a big waste of time. I felt like I was in Pre-K. I also felt stupid. Most of the work was in the workbook and most of what we did I already knew, so I didn't learn that much. Usually, we would play a game or just sit and wait for the time to pass. When we finished our work, we would sleep or go on the computers. We didn't have homework. When it was time to go the teacher just gave us candy." She tried to get out of ESL, "but the school wouldn't let me." She felt trapped. "Being non-American gets you put in ESL, no matter if you know English or not. Being Mexican kept me in ESL."

Sandra went on to say, "Occasionally when the other bilingual students were absent or not there for whatever reason, I would be pulled out at any time—whether it was during class, lunch, or even after school when I was in choir—to help translate between parents and teachers. I didn't mind at first; actually, I thought I was doing a good deed by helping. That was until I found out it was illegal. As a student my job is to learn, not to be a free translator for the convenience of the school."

Once Sandra entered high school, she felt that there was a lot of racial tension at her new school. "Students who are fluent English speakers would pick on or laugh at Asian or Latino students who are not fluent English speakers. I don't think teachers or the principal would do anything about it. No one I know has ever tried talking to teachers, counselors or the principal. You are kind of on your own for this situation." In addition, "Kids at school definitely laughed at Asian or Hispanic kids who went to the ESL class and said they talk funny or they need special help. One student in her school was speaking Viet [sic] with friends at lunch and other students would come over to them and say 'ching chong, ching chong,' which made them feel really bad about themselves."

In high school, Sandra was placed in ESL classes because the Vietnamese and Hispanic students were given forms for their parents to sign even though they never met with their parents to explain the purpose of the ESL classes. Even though the form said they had a right to refuse ESL classes, they felt that they did not have enough information to make that decision.

At Sandra's school there are no Spanish-speaking teachers. "My dad doesn't go to the school for parent-teacher conferences since the school doesn't reach out to communicate with my parents since they don't speak English, which creates a barrier for my parents to communicate with my teachers."

> "Students who are fluent English speakers would pick on or laugh at Asian or Latino students who are not fluent English speakers. I don't think teachers or the principal would do anything about it. No one I know has ever tried talking to teachers, counselors or the principal. You are kind of on your own for this situation."

What Needs to Change?

This scenario is not uncommon in many districts around the country, especially those districts that are experiencing rapid growth in the EL population and are unfamiliar with the legal requirements and instructional programs that would best serve their needs. The unintended consequences include ELs being "trapped in the system," as in the case of Sandra, thus creating a pipeline of permanent Long-Term English Learners (LTELs) who cannot exit after six or more years in ESL programs. As a result, they are unable to participate in core academic and college prep courses. ELs often report of "façade" learning environments that encourage playing on the computer, watching movies, and sleeping, rather than rigorous English-language instruction. ELs are also taught curriculum and instruction that are not aligned with their level of development, often leading to repetition and stagnation for students who should be at the intermediate and advanced levels (Olsen 2010).

Where educators address the SEL needs of LTELs and their innermost desire to belong, then LTELs no longer become withdrawn and suffer in silence but look up to the adults who are there to help them. This level of inclusion and responsiveness disrupts the pipeline that results in ELs becoming LTELs. Under normal circumstances, educating the whole child by striking a balance between the social, emotional, and academic expectations better prepares children to be successful in school, career, and in life. Creating both a work and learning environment that emphasizes social and emotional development is essential in order to have more inclusive practices that accelerate student learning and social integration that is more welcoming and rewarding.

With the increased focus on SEL, schools and school districts are now considering ways to assist ELs to successfully transition back into the mainstream of a school culture while responding equitably, fairly, and responsibly to the consequences of the break in educational structure, support, and adult role models as a result of the pandemic. Here are a few steps that would greatly enhance the transition and adaptation back to an altered learning environment.

1. Gain a clear understanding of the different characteristics and circumstances of ELs—not only their history, culture, language, and academic abilities but the trauma and scarcity that they may have experienced during the stay-at-home orders.
2. Become proficient in the competencies of social and emotional learning (SEL), pursue systemic implementation of SEL, and adapt a growth mind-set that looks at the potential and possibilities for all students rather than focusing on their deficits.
3. Become familiar and comfortable with cooperative, collaborative, and engaging instructional practices, although remotely or in class with social distancing, which give all students the opportunity to increase their social awareness and build positive relationships with children from different backgrounds.
4. Integrate EL academic and SEL strategies and methodologies systemically into the core operations of the school and in all learning platforms.

The research is conclusive that students who are exposed to explicit instruction of SEL competencies by teachers who model SEL and are given ample opportunities to practice and reinforce these competencies show greater academic gains, have positive feelings about school and adults in the school, have less disciplinary problems, and have reduced stress and anxiety (CASEL 2019a). This is why it is essential that school administrators model, facilitate, and support the full integration of social and emotional learning school wide with the added emphasis of embedding SEL in literacy strategies and academic language. The two are inseparable.

Time must be scheduled for teachers to collaborate, share data and instructional strategies, and support one another during these challenging and difficult times. Even though educators have commented that they are all "Zoomed out," administrators need to continue showing their support and motivation and modeling creative and effective ways to remain emotionally and socially connected to students even though they may be physically separated or practicing social distancing. This can be done by allocating resources, support, structure, and freedom to create; by taking risks in trying new approaches to addressing the needs of ELs; and by helping LTELs to overcome the cumulative academic deficits from years of being poorly assessed, misplaced in remedial classes, and having low expectations. The COVID Slide must not be an excuse for not addressing their academic deficiencies and frustration. Just as important, SEL needs to be modeled by the administrators, teachers, and support staff in treating all students and families with respect, concern, and empathy.

Diversity among ELs

English learners are a highly heterogeneous group, yet they usually wind up in the same ESL or sheltered instruction classroom, as was the case with Sandra (Olsen 2010). Schools need to be more proactive in identifying the language, literacy, and academic background of each student. Even though each student has unique experiences and there is great variation within each language and cultural group, the following are not fixed categories nor does it predict their future success in school and beyond. Most importantly, this information should be used in making "responsible decisions" as to what instructional interventions ELs need, whether they be Long-Term ELs (LTELs), highly Schooled Newcomers (HSN) Students with Interrupted Formal Education (SIFE) or students who have been traumatized by the pandemic.

1. **Striving Readers**—They may or may not be ELs. Many are English-speaking, native-born struggling readers. They have fallen through the cracks when it comes to developing those language and literacy skills. They need intensive intervention before they get too far behind.

2. **Long-Term ELs (LTELs)**—These students are primarily at the secondary level who have been in the system for six or more years, most of whom are born in the US. They may be able to carry on a conversation in English but are generally socially, psychologically, and academically isolated from the general student population and are behind academically. They are verbally proficient but cannot seem to meet the criteria for being reclassified or mainstreamed. Why are they so far behind? Factors include family circumstances, lack of academic rigor, low expectations, "dumbing down" of the curriculum, and being locked out of higher-level college prep courses while being tracked in the low-level sheltered English classes. They generally have not benefited from bilingual, ESL, pull-out, or even English immersion programs.

3. **Highly Schooled Newcomers (HSNs)**—These are newcomers who are highly schooled with strong literacy skills and know math, science, geography, and history in their native language and can benefit from accelerated language instruction. They may even be proficient in English. These students are *highly resourced*.

4. **Students with Interrupted Formal Education** (SIFEs)—These are students who come into our upper elementary, middle, and high schools with very little formal education. They have very low literacy levels even in their native language. Students with Interrupted Formal Education are also Newcomers. They have been in US schools less than two years. They are very likely reading at a K–2 level in English or in their primary language because they have had very little education or no education in their native country.

5. **Reclassified ELs (R-ELs)**—They may have met the benchmark and have English conversational skills but are not receiving any support or interventions as required by law to help them develop the academic language. They are struggling in all subject areas and are falling further behind as the content gets more difficult. They may be well behaved but are suffering in silence. Districts who receive federal funds have to provide tutorials and so forth.

6. **Migrant-ELs (M-ELs)**—They are constantly moving from place to place in search of jobs or better living conditions. They may become an LTEL or the valedictorian of the school.

7. **Special Education ELs** (SE-ELs)—They may have emotional and learning disabilities, speech, language, visual, and hearing impairments. But ELs are overrepresented in Special Education classes not due to learning disabilities but lack of English proficiency (Olsen 2010). Many are unaccompanied minors coming in from Central America. ELs must be evaluated in English and in their primary language. The problem is that it is difficult to evaluate in all the primary languages. Sometimes it is difficult to find the appropriate assessments and evaluators, even in more common languages such as Spanish. The ultimate responsibility is on the school district to find and hire the human resources and have the process and tools for different language groups.

Social and Emotional Learning (SEL)

Sandra's story unfortunately illustrates how adult values, behaviors, practices, and policies worked against ensuring a successful school experience for many ELs. The Five Core SEL Competencies (outlined below) serve as a compass to help guide decisions that are in the best interests of all students and adults. In an ideal school where SEL is fully implemented and with an equity focus, one would hope to see students who are highly proficient in English showing empathy and support for ELs and classroom environments that are inclusive, positive, and encouraging, and that foster respect and value diversity. This would be a school where teachers intentionally facilitate interaction and cooperation between students of all backgrounds and proficiency levels, create classrooms in which students are encouraged in every way and feel safe and free to take risks without fear of being ridiculed, teased, or ostracized. This school is full of praise, complements, and constructive feedback that serve to motivate and guide students to accelerate their academic achievement and social integration. However, a strong SEL program is still not enough for ELs if it is not integrated with the appropriate academic English language acquisition and course content knowledge necessary to graduate ready for college or career.

Developments in neuroscience and learning theory point to the fact that a greater emphasis on building a caring community of learners, coupled with high expectations and challenging and engaging opportunities in the classroom, results in students becoming more reflective of their own emotions and relationships (CASEL 2019). These conditions enhance students' motivation to learn, which is directly linked to academic success. School-based universal interventions and their effect in enhancing students' social and emotional learning supports the premise that cognitive, affective, and behavior skills are the foundation of academic success. In effect, students are more likely to express their creativity, curiosity, and empathy in environments where they feel included and safe. Students who have developed their SEL competencies will be better prepared for success in the 21st century.

Since the founding of the Collaborative for Academic, Social, and Emotional Learning (CASEL) in 1994 and the publication of Daniel Goleman's (1995) book *Emotional Intelligence*, the field of social and emotional learning in K–12 education has advanced exponentially. According to CASEL (2019), SEL seeks to:

foster the development of students who are actively engaged in learning; show caring and concern for the well-being of others; and demonstrate higher-order thinking, innovation, creativity and the ability to work toward common learning goals and contribute to the well-being of others and to their school community, all while making strong academic gains.

This is consistent with the primary goals set out by advocates and experts who focus on the needs of ELs.

It must be noted that ELs cannot participate fully in SEL practices that require English oral language discourse to express feelings and emotions unless the SEL practices are done in the primary language of the child or explicitly taught in the same manner as teaching academic vocabulary. ELs benefit greatly when they are able to collaborate with peers to learn academic language, express their feelings, and engage in meaningful activities.

Five Core SEL Competencies

Social and emotional learning involves processes through which children and adults develop fundamental emotional and social competencies to understand and manage emotions, set and achieve positive goals, feel and show empathy for others, establish and maintain positive relationships, and make responsible decisions (CASEL 2019a).

CASEL identifies five core SEL competencies that can help ELs strengthen their cognitive, affective, and behavior skills.

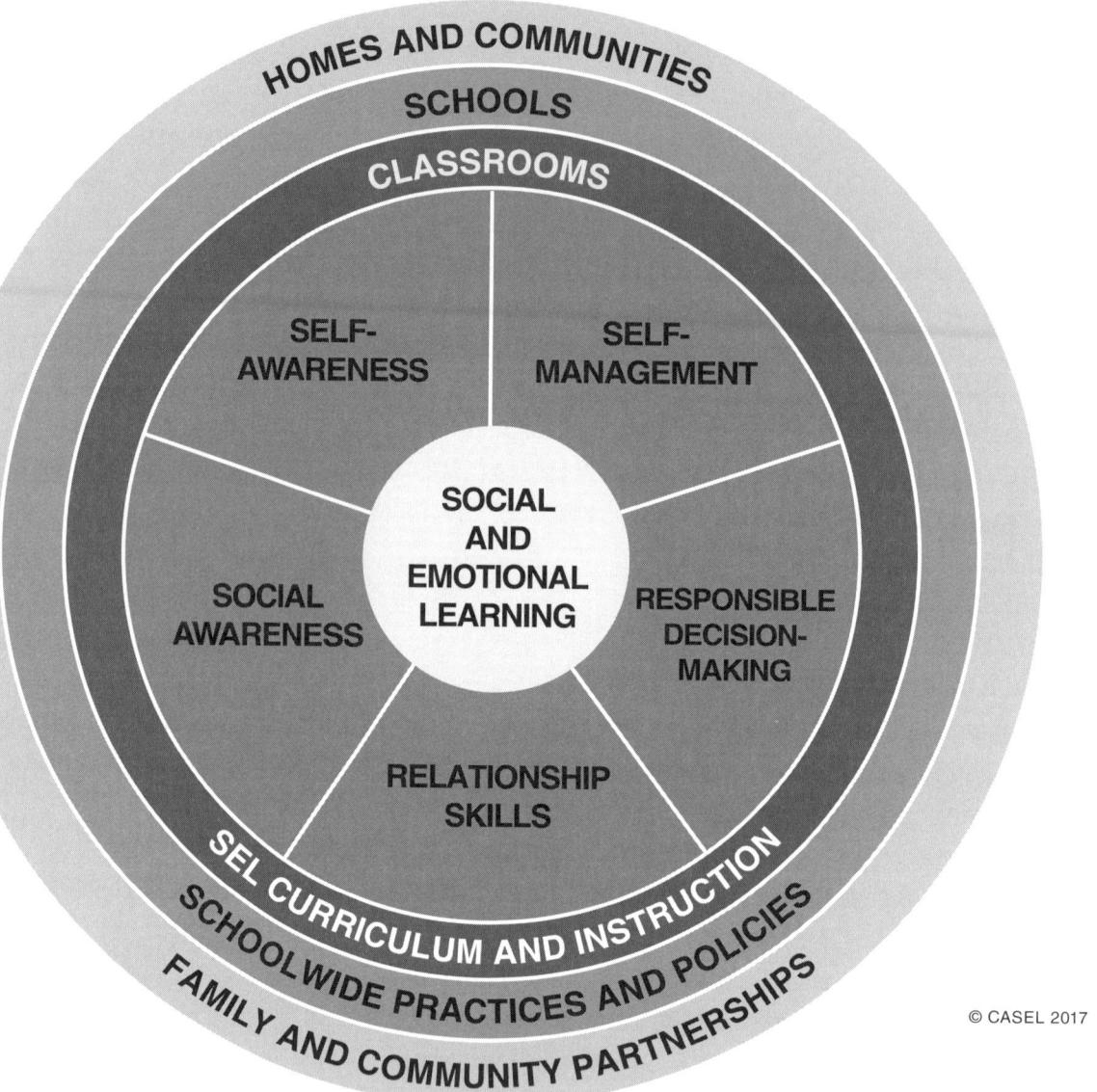

Source: CASEL 2019c
Figure 1.1 Five Core SEL competencies

© CASEL 2017

1. **Self-awareness:** This is the ability to accurately recognize one's feelings and thoughts and their influence on behaviors, which includes assessing one's strengths and limitations and possessing a well-grounded sense of self-efficacy and optimism.

2. **Self-management:** This is the ability to regulate one's emotions, thoughts, and behaviors effectively in different situations, which includes delaying gratification, managing stress, controlling impulses, motivating oneself, and setting and working toward achieving personal and academic goals.

3. **Social awareness:** This is the ability to take the perspective of, and empathize with others from diverse backgrounds and cultures, to understand social and ethical norms for behavior, and to recognize family, school, and community resources and supports.

4. **Relationship skills:** This is the ability to establish and maintain healthy and rewarding relationships with diverse individuals and groups, which includes communicating clearly, listening actively, cooperating, resisting inappropriate social pressure, negotiating conflict constructively, and seeking help when needed.

5. **Responsible decision-making:** This is the ability to make constructive choices about personal behavior, social interactions, and school, which includes considering ethical standards, safety concerns, social norms, the consequences of various actions, and the well-being of self and others. Responsible decisions reflect concern for one's well-being as well as the well-being of others.

Explicitly teaching social and emotional skills is essential to meeting many state academic standards, especially the Common Core Standards. For example, teaching students how to regulate their emotions, problem solve, disagree respectfully, collaborate with their peers, and see others' perspectives are meeting state standards for most core content. Thus, an SEL classroom with ELs is one in which teachers develop and maintain a safe, supportive, and well-managed learning environment where students feel cared for, respected, included in the conversation, and challenged academically. This is the type of classroom climate in which ELs flourish, socially, emotionally, and academically.

Empathy

For LTELs, one of the most important SEL competencies that should be addressed in schools and in the classroom is *empathy,* which is a component of Social Awareness of the Five Core SEL Competencies. A school community that takes the perspective of and empathizes with others from diverse backgrounds and cultures is one that establishes systems that welcome ELs and their families into the school, provides services in a friendly and culturally sensitive manner to ensure that the children receive appropriate placements, and trains teachers to be prepared to meet their needs. Being socially aware means that the school embraces the family as a valuable member of the community. This also means that the school strives to become knowledgeable of school and community resources that facilitate the ELs' transition into a new environment.

Empathizing with others from diverse backgrounds is both a complex concept and a difficult skill. In this era of high stakes testing and accountability, what is often referred to as soft skills, such as empathy, is not always valued, much less explicitly taught. To feel empathy toward others from different cultures and backgrounds requires one to not only take a critical look at one's own biases and prejudices but to consider what it takes to have a more empathetic mindset. Empathy involves celebrating, on a regular basis, the unique qualities and talents that each child brings to school and by acknowledging, validating, and embedding these unique qualities into the daily routines and practices of the classroom. Empathy is not allowing the LTEL to suffer in silence, be ignored, or to be looked at with disdain and resentment by their peers or even adults. It takes persistence, determination, and teamwork to keep empathy as the center of focus and not allow it to become replaced by cynicism, sarcasm, disparaging remarks, and neglect.

Empathy is the ability to accurately identify the emotional states of others and respond to them with care and concern. The story of Sandra certainly brings into focus the plight of many students who are "trapped in the system" without an advocate who is sensitive to the needs of ELs, thus resulting in the large number of ELs becoming LTELs. A school climate that is safe for students to ask for help does not happen by accident; it has to be cultivated intentionally. A "helping" curriculum addresses four basic questions:

1. Did you ask for help today when you needed it?
2. Did you offer help to another when you recognized that he or she needed it?
3. Do you accept help when it is offered to you?
4. If you declined help, did you do it politely? (Sapon-Shevin 2010)

These "helping behaviors" are essential components of a cooperative and inclusive classroom and school and are at the heart of a social and emotional learning environment. If taught explicitly and practiced regularly helping behaviors could be the catalyst that establishes and sustains a caring and safe classroom culture. These behaviors are essential for cooperative learning and group work to be successful. They are strategies that would help ELs to seek assistance to challenges that they face without embarrassment or ridicule. Helping strategies would also give English-dominant students the permission, the license, and inspiration to assist others, thus strengthening their SEL competencies such as empathy, compassion, and valuing of diversity. Modeling and facilitating empathy in the classroom are difficult but essential to creating an inclusive climate and culture that validates and excludes none. One specific and realistic way of helping ELs, for example, would be to help English-dominant students be more understanding of ELs' accents and not ridicule them, as was the case with the Vietnamese students in Sandra's story. ELs need to feel secure enough to raise their hands, take risks, and participate in class like everyone else.

Levels of School-Wide SEL

The most effective approach to make SEL systemic is to go school-wide. Integrating SEL fully with the academic program and across all systems, in preschool through high school, provides opportunities for

- Establishing a powerful, relationship-centered approach to education.
- Putting the social and emotional development of young people at the heart of every class room and school.
- Linking and integrating academic, social, and emotional learning in meaningful ways that support the full spectrum of students' development.
- Enhancing student learning by increasing students':
  1. Motivation to achieve.
  2. Ability to be attentive and engaged in the learning process.
  3. Satisfaction with learning.
  4. Sense of belonging.
- Fostering the development of essential life skills. (CASEL 2019a)

The Three Most Important Levels of SEL Implementation

1. **Classroom Level.** Classroom SEL is where explicit SEL skills instruction and a safe, nurturing, and inclusive learning climate with positive student–adult relationships are established. This is especially important for ELs and more so for LTELs. Teachers should not only teach SEL skills but encourage all, ELs and English-dominant students, to practice those skills throughout the day with one another and with adults. Another approach is to embed SEL instruction into content areas such as English as a second language (ESL), English language development (ELD), English language arts, social studies, science, and math. We have discussed embedding SEL competencies such as empathy and helpful behaviors into the instruction framework and have labeled these as beneficial strategies in helping ELs transition

quickly into the culture and academic milieu of mainstream society. We will later see a few examples of mindfulness exercises, cooperative learning activities, and cultural responsiveness practices with an academic focus.

2. **School Level.** At the building level is where SEL becomes embedded into the core functioning of the school's culture, climate, practices, and policies. A safe and positive school climate is recognized as an important factor for improving academic, behavioral, and mental health outcomes for students. A sense of trust among students, families, and school staff is one dimension of climate that is particularly important for promoting adult and student SEL. Unfortunately, this is not always the case, especially for ELs and their families. Principals and school leaders can organize building-level strategies that build positive relationships and a sense of community intentionally and by design with a special emphasis on students and families of ELs. Administrators and teachers can also establish procedures within the school or even remotely, such as Norms of Virtual Collaboration and the way that staff meetings are conducted, to help support the practice of SEL competencies. Feeling socially, emotionally, and physically safe is another important climate characteristic that supports social and emotional development and is critical for the success of LTELs. School-wide practices and policies that promote this type of school environment often reap the benefits of an aligned SEL system where students are exposed to multiple years of SEL practice and integration and actively engage in assisting ELs and LTELs.

3. **Parent and Family Level.** Parents and schools working together to build the social, emotional, and academic skills of all students can accomplish far more than working alone. Both schools and parents can contribute in unique ways to make sure that ELs and especially LTELs are successful academically and integrated socially. Families that are welcomed into the school should also be offered opportunities to learn about how SEL is being practiced in the classroom and be trained on how to extend SEL into the home. This means offering SEL in a language and in a cultural context that parents can understand and relate to. Families and community partners can help extend SEL into community-based organizations, health care providers, governmental agencies, and other community institutions. It is also important for staff to help parents understand the importance and connections of SEL with academic achievement, emotional well-being, and the acquisition of English for their children.

Parent Support and Engagement

For the most part, teachers are very passionate about wanting to engage families but often admit that they don't know how to, especially if the families are non-English speaking. They need help in understanding the culture and communicating in the language that the parents and guardians understand. Reaching out to parents of ELs, and engaging families makes their job easier, not harder. The investment in the beginning can be time-consuming, especially because teachers already have so much on their plates.

Once *open and trusting communications* have been established between the home and school, this is a window of opportunity for teachers, counselors, and administrators to get to the heart of the challenges that LTELs face at school and personally. The pain of feeling excluded, the emotional cost of failure, and the shame that is often the consequence of exclusion, ridicule, and bullying, take an emotional toll over time. Parental relationships and interactions with children can help children grow emotionally and give them confidence to seek out help when needed.

In spite of the many challenges in the home and at work, parents also need *help with understanding the positive impact* that social and emotional learning can have on the family and their children's ability to cope with stress and disappointment. Empathic listening is an SEL skill that parents can begin in the home by listening to their children's personal stories of success and pain in school and in relationships. Telling their story to their parents creates opportunities to address difficult or hurtful emotions, to explore the true nature of those feelings, and to consider how to work with them constructively. Parents can encourage children to use feeling words, such as, "I feel sad," or, "That made me really angry," to express their emotions rather than simply act on them.

Helping children to develop good social and emotional skills early in life makes a big difference to their long-term health and well-being. If children learn to express emotions constructively and engage in caring and respectful relationships before and while they are in their lower elementary grades, they are more likely to avoid depression, violence, and other serious mental health problems as they grow older. Children's success in school and life greatly depends on how they become aware and manage intense feelings, whether of joy or grief or fear. Parents need help recognizing when their children are upset and how to help their children manage stressors and even trauma related to arguments or homework, or life-altering realities such as parental divorce, economic hardship, family moves, uncertainties of immigration status, illness or death of loved ones related to the pandemic or other tragedies, and the impact that it has on their emotions and learning. Stress and its emotional consequences may be unavoidable, but expressing emotions in healthy ways means that children can deal with the pressures of life with much greater strength, wisdom, and resilience.

Schools and parents, working together, can play pivotal roles in supporting *children's healthy development* in dealing with their emotions and in their relationships with others. When social and emotional skills are taught and mastered, they help students to succeed not just in school but in all avenues of life. Numerous studies have found that young people who possess these social and emotional skills are in fact happier, more confident, and more capable as students, family members, friends, and workers. Social and emotional learning is a powerful way to help children become healthy, caring, and competent. In the case of LTELs, the more that parents are informed and trained in SEL competencies and skills, the better their children will be able to overcome challenges, and instead of personal resignation, they will be empowered and more confident in seeking help, setting personal goals, and overcoming the systemic barriers that have been placed before them.

When parents and students practice and use SEL skills at home, the effects are doubly beneficial. Not only are young people better able to acquire the skills, but relationships within the family tend to improve when family members listen to one another openly and solve problems together. Children also come to appreciate the fact that learning is a lifelong process, not only in school but in the home as well.

It is not enough that parents receive training in SEL competencies, tools, and strategies to be used at home; they also need *support from one another*. This is where the school can play a significant role in facilitating parent-to-parent networking so that they have an extended family around them to offer advice or share in the tasks of raising children. Parents of ELs often feel isolated, lonely, and overwhelmed. When parents have the opportunity to meet with and learn from a skilled teacher as well as from one another, they can share the problems they experience with their children and learn ways of working through them. They learn that they are not the only ones experiencing certain problems with their children, and that there are creative and constructive options for addressing them. When a group of parents agree to support one another in setting household rules, such as limiting time in front of the television or establishing regular times for homework, it is much more likely that those rules will be enforced by adults and obeyed by children. This slight change in parent networking practice can produce infinite possibilities for ELs by helping them help their children further develop their social, emotional, and academic skills.

One proven way to strengthen the relationship between parents and schools is through *family-school teams*. These typically include parents, teachers, and school administrators where they work collaboratively to make decisions about designing and implementing programs, often for parent involvement and student support. When parents are actively involved in making decisions about school practices that benefit their children, then they and other parents enjoy programs and activities that truly address their needs. And when parents and teachers work closely together, then students hear the same messages at home and school about acceptable behavior and the importance of studying and learning and ways that they can overcome the plight of LTELs. Having common expectations makes it far easier for LTELs to succeed academically, for schools to be more understanding and responsive, and for teachers to be more empathetic, compassionate, and able to make responsible decisions that correct the systemic deficiencies that may have caused ELs to become LTELs.

Many parents feel unsure of their own parenting abilities and helpless in the face of the negative influences in spite of the fact that children want their parents to be there guiding them and teaching them. For the most part, young people feel that their parents are very important influences on their lives. When families and schools work together, the benefits for students, academically, socially, and emotionally, are magnified. Involved parents tend to be more confident in making decisions about their family and enjoy being with their children more; they are more sensitive to their children's social, emotional, and intellectual needs; and they are more affectionate and restorative and used less punishment with their children

In *raising caring, confident, capable children*, here are ten suggestions that parents can do at home to teach their children social and emotional skills and give them greater strength, wisdom, and resilience in dealing with life's pressures (CASEL 2019c).

1. Focus on strengths. When children bring home a test, first praise what they did well and then talk about what can be improved. Do not just criticize items that were wrong. This may be especially true for LTELs who have had years of failure and setbacks. This is the perfect time to build confidence. Shaming has never been a motivator to do better.

2. Follow up with fair consequences for misbehavior. Sometimes parents/caregivers demand unfair consequences in anger. "Because of what you did, no television for a month." Set fair consequences and consistently carry them out, focusing on the behavior and not the person, keeping in mind that, in the end, there needs to be a time to reconnect and repair the relationship.

3. Ask children how they feel. When parents show interest in their child's feelings and challenges, they are sending the message that their feelings matter and that the parent cares. Most importantly, when parents ask this question, then empathic listening and nonjudgmental silence on the part of the parent is the most effective strategy in helping children process their emotions and make sense out of their experiences.

4. Find ways to stay calm when angry. Know it is normal to get angry or irritated, but parents should not lose control. Instead, take a few deep breaths, or just stop talking, or leave the room. Encourage family discussion about what everyone can do to stay calm.

5. Avoid humiliating or mocking your child. Unfair criticism and sarcasm can make children feel badly about themselves. They can lose confidence, which can cause illness and problems with schoolwork and getting along with friends. It also weakens parents' mutual bond of trust. LTELs have had enough disappointments and rejection in the schools and social circles; they do not need additional put downs in the home. Try to give children room to make mistakes when they are learning new skills.

6. Be willing to apologize. When there is miscommunication, parents should be the first to apologize and calmly explain what they really meant. Being a good role model means teaching that it is possible to work through problems with consideration and respect for others. LTELs need parents/caregivers as partners who are transparent and share in the healing process while repairing the relationship.

7. Give children choices and respect their wishes. When children have a chance to make choices, they learn how to solve problems. Letting children make decisions teaches them that their ideas and feelings matter. This is when parents can provide the most guidance. LTELs would greatly benefit in having parents assist them in reflecting on their current

circumstances, identifying and managing their emotions, and making decisions that would effectively address challenges that have held them back.

8. Ask questions that help children solve problems on their own. When children have a problem, parents *should not* step in and take over. Instead, they should try to ask good questions and encourage their children to find their own appropriate solutions that address immediate difficulties but have long-term positive consequences on overall goals and desires for their futures.

9. Read books and stories together. Reading aloud, especially in their native language, is a way to share something enjoyable and learn how other people deal with common issues in a number of cultures, like making or losing friends or handling conflicts.

10. Encourage sharing and helping. There are many ways to do this. Together parents and their children can prepare food in a homeless shelter, go on a fundraising walk-a-thon, help out elderly neighbors, or offer aid to needy families. This teaches children that what they do can make a difference in the lives of others. For LTELs, this activity of giving and serving the community gives them a greater sense of purpose outside of school and has the potential to shape and motivate them to set and achieve academic goals and pursue future career goals.

Conclusion

In this chapter we have taken a closer look at the plight of LTELs and how social and emotional learning in the context of the school, classroom, and home can contribute to the success of LTELs. Through the systemic implementation of SEL and the Five SEL Core Competencies, schools and school districts are in the position of providing LTELs a ray of hope that they desperately need. Addressing the harmful effects of segregated ESL and language acquisition systems requires an added focus and practice of the SEL competencies of Social-Awareness, Relationship Skills and most importantly Responsible Decision Making. This must be done systemically and systematically at the classroom, school, and district levels. Recruiting parents to become active co-creators of effective strategies to resolve this problem is essential in discontinuing the practices that create LTELs. Perhaps through these efforts, together we can eliminate future scenarios that typify the destiny of ELs like Sandra.

Personal Reflections and Collegial Discussions

1. Which SEL competencies are needed to eliminate the practices that contribute to the creation of LTELs?

   _____

2. How can SEL contribute to greater inclusion practices for ELs, cultural awareness, and culturally responsive teaching that ultimately benefits LTELs?

   _____

3. How can SEL be used to enhance academic achievement for LTELs?

   _____

4. How can professional development on SEL and intentional practices help adults develop their SEL competencies when addressing the systemic exclusion of ELs?

   _____

5. How would SEL practices be manifested in school-related activities, events, meetings, and over-all climate and culture of the school in order to eliminate the achievement gaps with LTELs?

   _____

6. Once adults have developed SEL skills and have become familiar with SEL-related activities, how would you ensure that they were being implemented into the daily practices of a school and the classrooms that would ultimately benefit LTELs?

   _____

7. How would you monitor and measure the effectiveness of integrating SEL skills and strategies with teaching academic language to ELs?

   _____

8. What would be your next steps in increasing parent training and engagement in addressing their children's classification as LTELs?

   _____

Chapter 2

Integrating SEL into a Mixed Learning Environment

We are all anxious, concerned, a bit apprehensive, yet excited about seeing students again. This makes the need for integrating social and emotional learning even more critical than ever before. While teachers are learning, experimenting, and taking risks with ways to effectively communicate with their students, particularly with LTELs, they are now having to deal with an entirely new way of teaching, interacting, maintaining student attention, and instructing.

As everyone struggles to make meaning of this new reality, teachers will need the support of their colleagues and administrators in order to help them take care of their mental health, better manage their workload, regulate their stress level, boost morale, and place their own well-being as a priority. It is not uncommon to hear reports that teachers are experiencing sadness, fear, uncertainty, and in a growing number of cases, burnout. Expressions such as being "Zoomed out" and "overwhelmed" are indicative of the difficulty of transitioning to new ways of being, teaching, and learning. But the more that teachers collaborate, the more confident they will feel that they will not have to go it alone. The more that the school leadership team reaches out to their staff the more prepared they will be to better serve the children. A new design of professional development is urgently needed that addresses the need to transition to a variety of delivery systems and classroom arrangements while acknowledging the steep learning curve that teachers have no option but to climb. It is our hope that you will find suggestions in this book for planning your professional development.

Theories and research about school and classroom climate, structure, management, and purpose are now being rewritten. What will the classroom look like now that social distancing is expected, wearing

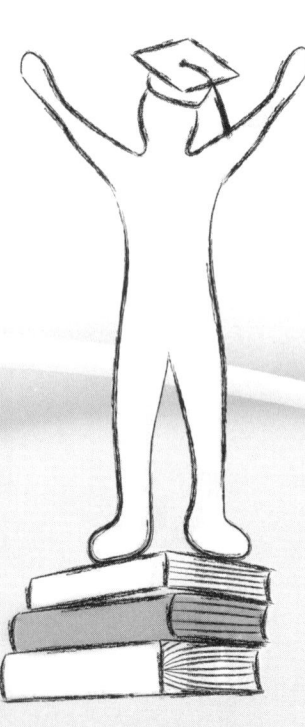

masks has become the new normal, and remote learning has made its way to becoming a significant part of the instructional delivery systems and adult planning and training? What does the school look like now that virtual or hybrid schools are replacing traditional structures of brick and mortar? The roles of the principals, counselors, coaches, and teachers are being redefined daily. How will instructional coaches support teachers?

These are critical questions that all educators are grappling to answer. There are challenges such as disparities between resources and scarcity, connectivity and disconnection, fear and anxiety for health concerns, and safety coupled with the uncertainty of ever "getting back to normal." Educators, politicians, businesses, and communities at all levels are having to come to terms with the stress, anxiety, trauma, and mental health issues that the current state of the pandemic, unemployment, and social unrest are having on adults and children. This makes the focus on embedding social and emotional learning into academics even more essential.

Each SEL competency focuses on specific "actions, attitudes and skills" that helps adults and students successfully handle daily challenges. Connecting the core competencies with specific circumstances is often difficult to do but here are a few thoughts on how the knowledge and practice of SEL skills and competencies can help mitigate the pressures, anxiety, and disappointment associated with transitioning to a new way of being and managing one's responsibilities (CASEL 2019c).

Self-Awareness is the ability to accurately recognize one's feelings and thoughts and their influence on behaviors, which includes assessing one's strengths and limitations and possessing a well-grounded sense of self-efficacy and optimism.

Figure 2.1: Definition of self-awareness

When the call went out to reopen schools during the pandemic, there was an immediate demand from educators that school districts ensure that every precaution was taken to guarantee that their health and safety were of highest priority. This increased the level of fear, anxiety, and stress among adults about the risk of exposure to children who may be asymptomatic but carriers of COVID-19. Coupled with the transition to remote learning and having to learn a new medium for delivering instruction has magnified the negative impact of stress and anxiety on adults' emotional well-being. In effect, teachers are currently under duress. That is, many teachers have surpassed the capacity to cope with the stress and the demands of the job and of life, threats on their job stability, or action by someone to do something against their will or better judgment such as teaching in the classroom.

Prior to the pandemic educators were already experiencing high levels of job-related stress and anxiety. Why are teachers feeling so stressed? While most educators report having control over classroom-level decisions, like teaching techniques and homework and grading policies, they have less influence over schoolwide decisions. Most teachers have minor or no influence over school budget decisions, nearly half have little or no say in determining professional development content, and many have minor or no influence in establishing curriculum at their schools. In a study of nearly 8,000 educators across the US, teachers were asked, "How do you feel each day at school?" The top three emotions reported were frustration, stress, and feeling overwhelmed. When asked how they want to feel at school each day, educators wrote in their own words: joyful, happy, excited, appreciated, supported, and energized (Forum 2019). If this was the case in 2017, we can imagine how teachers feel in 2021.

A recent survey of teens by the Pew Research Center revealed that *anxiety and depression top the list of problems that teens see among their peers* (Menasce Horwitz, Graf 2019). Of those polled 70 percent felt that anxiety and depression were a "major problem," while 26 percent felt that it was a minor problem. This ranked above bullying (55 percent), drug addiction (51 percent), and drinking alcohol (45 percent). These are pre-pandemic statistics. Estimates are that these figures are much higher now than two years ago.

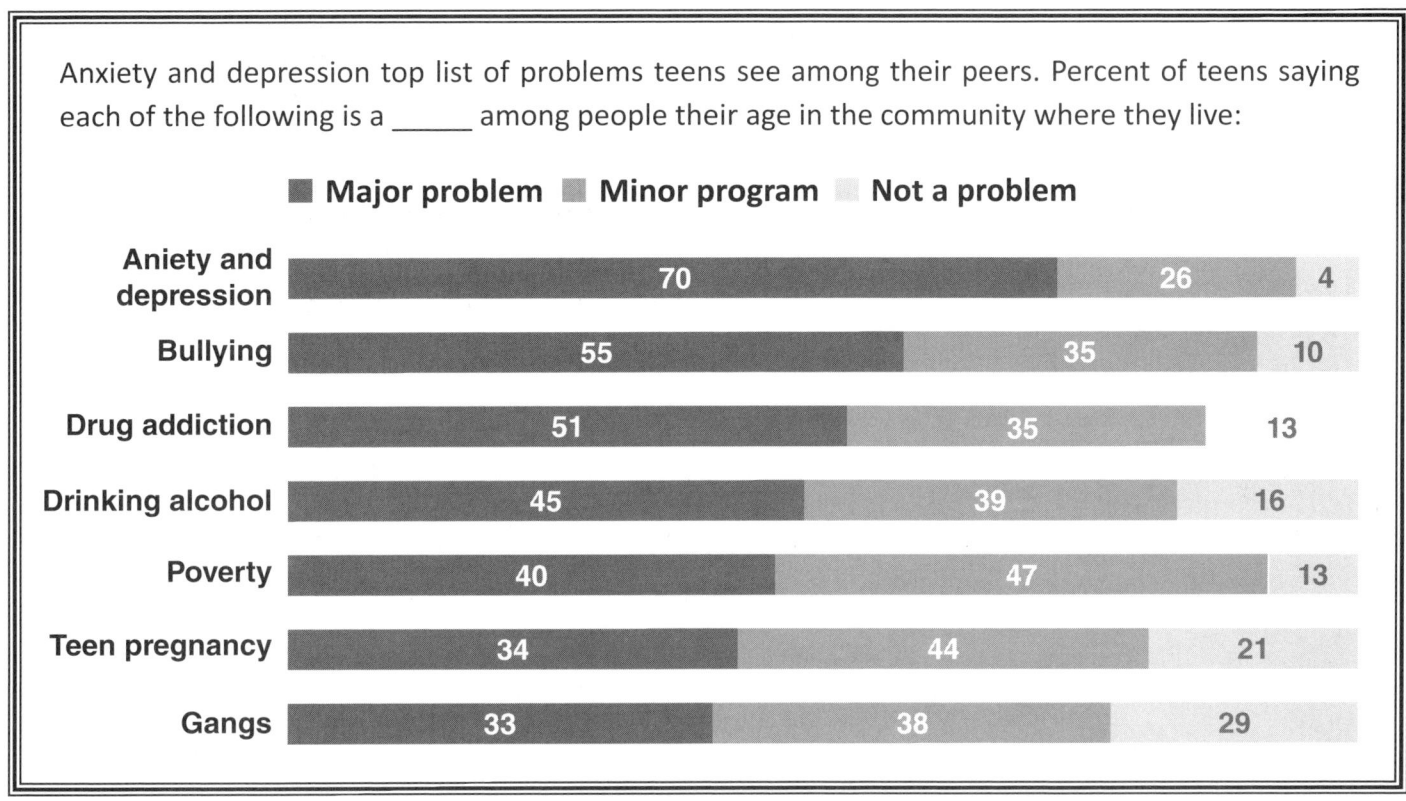

Figure 2.2 Anxiety and depression among teens (Menasce Horwitz, Graf 2019)

Since teachers cannot expect to "pick up where they left off" they are being called on to exhibit a higher degree of empathy, compassion, and flexibility while being in touch with their emotions so as not to be overwhelmed by the challenges of dealing with students' emotional difficulties, learning new skills, and experiencing disappointment. The ability to properly identify one's emotions and have an accurate self-perception go hand in hand with recognizing strengths and building self-confidence and self-efficacy. Adults who are "in touch with their emotions" are in a better position to guide the students to assess their own emotions as well.

Teachers who have taken the time to become more self-aware know that their students will need assistance to be in touch with their emotions since they have experienced months of separation from peers and adult contact other than immediate family. The break from face-to-face social connectivity that was replaced with electronic interfacing made it difficult to provide adult modeling and reinforcement of positive social and communication skills. Teachers and administrators were having enough difficulties transitioning to new virtual platforms, programs, apps, and standards, but when adults are transparent with students, the students have a better sense that they are not the only ones who may be struggling with their emotions.

However, being transparent with students is not sufficient to help them identify emotions that should lead them to regulate and manage them more effectively. Throughout the nation, teachers, administrators, school districts, and states are realizing that good intentions need to be guided by a set of clear SEL standards that provide direction for teachers to narrow the field of SEL competencies to teach students. Explicit instruction of SEL competencies helps students develop social and emotional learning skills that will put them on the road to a bright future. There are many excellent examples of SEL standards ranging from K-12 that have been developed by districts and can be found in the District Resource Center at CASEL.org.

In the area of Self Awareness several recurring themes across a number of examples of SEL standards have emerged but differ on the depth of implementation depending on age and grade level. Since our focus is on LTELs, these examples represent Standards, Indicators, and Activities at the secondary level.

Competency: Self Awareness

Standard	Indicator	Activities
1A –Recognize and identify emotions to demonstrate personal responsibility	Individual demonstrates an understanding of personal emotions.	Students make a poster or draw a picture that depicts a range of their emotions under certain circumstances. Look at ways in history that various characters have communicated their emotions and discuss the results.
	Individual demonstrates an awareness of personal actions.	Students role play and discuss situations that might trigger emotions.
1B—Demonstrate an accurate self-concept based on one's strengths and challenges	Individual demonstrates knowledge of personal strengths and potential.	Students do a "show and tell" presentation about a hobby or a skill.
	Individual is able to describe personal interests, qualities, and strengths that may help with decision-making to accomplish personal goals.	As a class, design a "movie set" city street with different storefronts. Each student designs a storefront that shares characteristics of themselves that can and cannot be changed.
1C—Identify personal, cultural, and linguistic assets	Individual demonstrates awareness of personal qualities.	Students create timelines that tell their own history. They should include five or six important events they remember throughout their lives.
	Individual embraces personal, cultural, and linguistic assets.	Students draw portraits of themselves and label them with skills, talents, languages they speak, and cultural traits they possess.
1D—Identify awareness of external supports	Individual identifies an adult they can trust.	Students explain situations in which they would need to seek adult help from someone whom they can trust with both big and small problems.
		Students identify the different school and community sources to which they could turn to get help for a number of needs such as academic, personal health, counseling, and family needs.

Source: SEL standards and indicators are adopted from the Anchorage School District, Oakland Unified School District PreK– Adult Social and Emotional Learning Standards and El Paso Learning Standards.

Table 2.1 Recognizing one's emotions, values, strengths, and challenges

The effective implementation of SEL Standards and Activities at any time and especially virtually is largely governed by the teacher's level of familiarity with the standards, their ability to navigate the restrictions of distance learning or the functions of the application used to connect with students remotely, and level of integration with the content being taught. Normally, this is a difficult task, but with persistence and administrative and collegial support the approach to connecting with students will improve.

Helping students be in touch with their feelings and emotions is essential when working with students at any time, especially remotely, through a hybrid or blended format, or face-to-face. It may take months if not years for the effects of the pandemic to subside. Meanwhile, there needs to be regular check-ins with students to help them process and manage emotions.

The resource that teachers are beginning to use more frequently is the Mood Meter developed by the Yale Center for Emotional Intelligence. If done remotely, as students come online at the beginning of a class, they enter in the color of their mood in the chat box and then complete the assessment again at the end of the class.

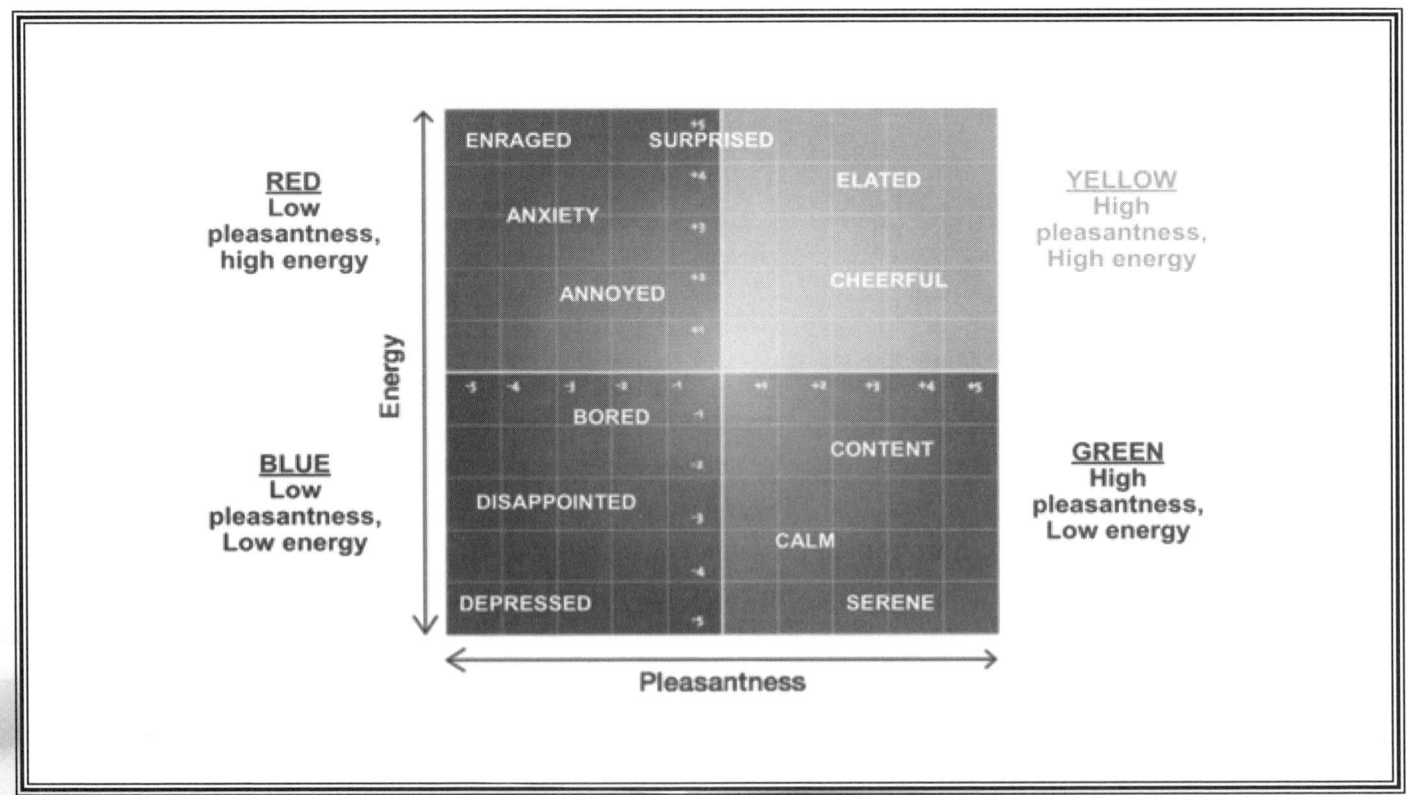

Figure 2.3 Mood Meter: Yale Center for Emotional Intelligence (Brackett 2019)

This gives the teacher a good read on how the students are feeling and the level of self-awareness of their emotions as well as providing feedback on how well a lesson may have impacted on their emotions and sense of belonging. It is also a good resource to help students to label their emotions, increase vocabulary, and inform the teacher of any adjustments that need to be made on the lesson and delivery for the following day.

Figure 2.4 Mood Meter: Yale Center for Emotional Intelligence (Brackett 2019)

This exercise has the potential to go beyond the superficial "How are you feeling?" activity. With the use of breakout rooms during live online classes, students have the opportunity to interact by discussing their emotions and the reasons behind their ratings and by developing positive relationships with other students. This would be especially beneficial for ELs and LTELs when it comes to establishing friendships, using oral language, and being more reflective on their feelings, thoughts, and emotions.

Self-Management: This is the ability to regulate one's emotions, thoughts, and behaviors effectively in different situations, which includes delaying gratification, managing stress, controlling impulses, motivating oneself, and setting and working toward achieving personal and academic goals.

Figure 2.5 Definition of self-management

One of the biggest challenges that teachers are facing is the ability to effectively interact with students the way they did prior to the pandemic. Even the general practice of group discussions and collaboration have become much more difficult, and in many preliminary findings, the virtual platform is proving to be much more complicated and less successful.

Teachers were taught, trained, and have taught in face-to-face and in-person learning environments. Now all that prior learning has been totally redefined without their consent, without having collaboratively decided on the degree, magnitude, and timeline of the change much less having a say on the equipment and programs to be used. Any hopes that the standard curriculum, lesson plans, and classroom management strategies will be effective in remote learning or with social distancing in class have been greatly reduced. In effect, teachers are like fish out of water. They were trained to swim; now they are being asked to run.

How can teachers make the best of the situation? This is new territory for all educators and the research is lacking but there seems to be emerging a number of promising practices that may contribute to the success of the virtual, hybrid, and social distancing learning environment. The more that teachers are able to become familiar with the fine nuances of remote controls and can practice interfacing with a number of web-based programs and implementing newly defined strategies, the better.

Focusing on Self-Management with students would be considered a high priority during these difficult times. However, adults also need to be able to manage stress and motivate themselves to set and achieve work-related goals of learning a new way of teaching and interacting with students. This is where a greater focus on a growth mindset for adults will directly benefit students.

Competency: Self-Management

Handling our emotions so they facilitate rather than interfere with the task at hand; being conscientious and delaying gratification to pursue goals; persevering in the face of setbacks and frustrations.

Standard	Indicator	Activities
2A—Use effective decision-making skills to regulate one's emotions and manage stress appropriately	Individual applies strategies to manage stress and to motivate successful performance.	Discuss the strategies that literary characters used to handle their stressors.
	Individual demonstrates ability to be self-disciplined, resulting in perseverance and resiliency.	Students develop a graphic organizer that compares and contrasts ways to express feelings.
2B—Motivate oneself to set and achieve attainable goals that result in school and life success	Individual utilizes appropriate organizational skills and tools to set, monitor, adapt, achieve, and evaluate goals.	Students watch or read culturally relevant literature and discuss the results of the characters' impulsive actions.
	Individual practices strategies for coping with and overcoming feelings of rejection, social isolation, and other forms of stress.	Trace the feet of students. On each footprint, students write a strategy for coping. Display as "steps to overcoming."
2C—Effectively participate in group decision-making processes	Individual demonstrates the skills to manage and express one's emotions, thoughts, impulses, and stress in constructive ways while working in a cooperative learning setting.	Practice win–win problem-solving strategies
	Individual demonstrates the ability to practice win–win problem-solving strategies.	Assign group work and ensure that all students are active participants

Source: SEL standards and indicators are adopted from the Anchorage School District, Oakland Unified School District PreK– Adult Social and Emotional Learning Standards and El Paso Learning Standards.

Table 2.1 Recognizing one's emotions, values, strengths, and challenges

Growth Mindset

The concept of a growth mindset is the idea that, with effort, it is possible to increase intelligence levels, talents, and abilities (Dweck 2016). But teachers cannot do it alone. With sustained, ongoing professional development that is linked to new classroom practices, teachers are more likely to see meaningful changes in their practices. Research on effective professional development suggests that for teachers to successfully change their practices in ways that lead to meaningful change in student outcomes, teachers need time, opportunities to practice, feedback, and institutional support. The priority should be on adults reconnecting and supporting one another and the sharing of practices, resources, and technology skills to navigate new instructional delivery systems, strategies, and approaches. One-shot professional learning workshops rarely lead to effective, sustained changes because they do not offer teachers opportunities to practice the new skills and get feedback.

In comparison, a Fixed Mindset is the belief that intelligence and talents are static, leading teachers to believe that their potential for success is based on whether they currently possess the required abilities to make a smooth transition to distance learning and remote classroom management. It has become increasingly evident that some educators have been tempted to give up when things become difficult, tend to avoid challenges hoping for things to get back to normal, see mistakes as failures, or approach success differently to their colleagues with a growth mindset.

Students need adults to model a growth mindset because students who demonstrate a growth mindset believe their abilities will develop over time, tend to seek out opportunities to gain new knowledge and broaden their skills, and do not typically shy away from challenges (Kazakoff and Mitchell 2017). Students with a growth mindset believe that they can learn to complete tasks, solve complex problems, or grow their intelligence, rather than assuming they "can" or "cannot" do something based on their current abilities. Having a growth mindset is essential to lifelong success, and it is something that students can develop with practice. There is a direct correlation between what a teacher thinks, models, and expects from a student and what a student thinks about their abilities and their level of achievement. For LTELs a greater focus on a growth mindset has the potential to help them overcome years of disappointment, failure, low self-confidence, and lack of self-esteem and helps them possess higher levels of self-confidence and motivation to learn.

By making changes in instructional practices, educators can foster an environment in which students are not only aware of the characteristics of a growth mindset but can actively take part in creating such a change of thinking. Here are a few steps in helping ELs and LTELs develop a growth mindset either in the classroom or remotely:

1. Read books with characters from their own background who have faced challenges and developed strategies to overcome them.

2. Conduct activities that give ELs the chance to practice phrases that promote growth mindset.

3. Display visible reminders on the screen of growth-mindset vocabulary using inspirational posters and anchor charts.

4. Have students work in pairs or in small groups in breakout rooms to discuss the qualities of a growth mindset and then submit growth mindset exit tickets either on Google Docs or on other platforms.

5. When giving feedback to students, use vocabulary and prompts that facilitate a growth mindset.

6. Model growth mindset as an educator.

Social Awareness is the ability to take the perspective of and empathize with others from diverse backgrounds and cultures, to understand social and ethical norms for behavior, and to recognize family, school, and community resources and supports.

Figure 2.6 Definition of social awareness

Many LTELs were already struggling academically and socially before the pandemic forced us to become even more isolated. Many students who are undocumented, ELs, disabled, having to work to support the family, and homeless are more likely to be disconnected from the school, experience overcrowding in the home, and food insecurities. These circumstances will further contribute to the existing inequities, achievement gap, and dropout rate. In effect, the infrastructure that normally supported basic needs is disintegrating for many families who live in poverty. Teachers themselves need to stay healthy, become more proficient in the new technology and equip themselves with intervention strategies that are effective in a virtual or mixed-learning environment. Students will be crying out for help, and the best strategies to meet their needs are deeply embedded in the core competencies of SEL.

In strengthening their abilities to model Social-Awareness, teachers are in a better position to teach, model, reinforce, and facilitate the practice of showing and feeling empathy for students who are without computers, connectivity, and adult support. As a teacher of content and a facilitator of interaction, teachers are in the position to create a learning environment where students who are better resourced can practice the art of compassion and kindness especially toward ELs.

Competency: Social Awareness

Understanding what others are feeling; being able to take their perspective;
appreciating and interacting positively with diverse groups.

Standard	Indicator	Activities
3A—Establish and maintain healthy interactions and relationships by embracing the perspectives of people different from oneself across diverse communities.	Individual demonstrates an awareness of cultural factors and respect for individual differences.	Give teams a list of emotions, cultural traits, and artifacts. They must design skits using all the characteristics and list of emotions given. The opposite team tries to guess what was on their list.
	Individual demonstrates empathy for other people's emotions, perspectives, cultures, languages, and histories.	Read the first half of a story that represents the culture and language of the students. After one character's actions, students predict how the other characters will feel.
3B—Demonstrate awareness of other people's emotions and perspectives to those similar and different from oneself.	Individual demonstrates consideration for others and a desire to contribute to the well-being of the school and community.	Hold class meetings and community circles where students are given the opportunity to learn about themselves, their differences, and ways to support one another, especially if they are made fun of.
	Individual demonstrates an awareness of cultural issues and a respect for human dignity and differences.	On the outside of a paper bag, students make a collage of how they think others feel about an issue, and on the inside, they put pictures/words of how they feel about that issue. Discuss.
3C—Develop social awareness skills needed to establish and maintain positive relationships	Individual recognizes leadership qualities in self and others and contributes productively to the school, workplace, and community.	Students participate in a clothing drive, food drive, or other service, and then follow through with the story by seeing how their contribution made an impact. Write a follow-up article discussing this impact and evaluating what they would do the same or what they could do differently.
	Individual can read social cues and respond appropriately.	Students identify the verbal and nonverbal cues that make a teacher-told story interesting. Discuss how different classmates might tell the story differently.
3D—Identify prejudices and biases towards people different than oneself.	Individual demonstrates an understanding of others' differences.	Ask students to write a list of traits that they have. Then go around the room comparing traits with their classmates.
	Individual demonstrates acceptance of others who are different	Distribute magazines that reflect different cultural interests. Students work in small groups to look for commonalities.

Source: SEL standards and indicators are adopted from the Anchorage School District, Oakland Unified School District PreK–Adult Social and Emotional Learning Standards and El Paso Learning Standards.

Table 2.3 SEL standards and competencies for Social Awareness

Culturally responsive approaches are also important to instructional practices for ELs. *Culturally responsive* teaching has been defined as using the cultural characteristics, experiences, and perspectives of ethnically diverse students as a means for teaching them more effectively (Jagers, Rivas-Drake, and Borowski 2018). Researchers describe three themes that can be used as a framework to enhance teachers' cultural responsiveness.

1. ***Multicultural awareness*** requires a teacher to increase awareness of his or her own biases and assumptions about the culture, language, and behavior of students.

2. ***Multicultural knowledge*** refers to acquiring knowledge of the particular students with whom teachers and other school staff work with. It is recommended that teachers actively try to learn about the cultural background of each of their students, including values they have that help shape the ways they deal with feelings, conflict, social interactions, social norms, and their individual learning styles. Talk with ELs, have them share experiences, and do more research on their history and culture. One especially important and effective way to get to know about the family and culture are home visits.

Figure 2.7 Valuing diversity of history, personal story and traditions
(3rd Grade Class, Austin, TX)

3. ***Multicultural skills*** are culturally appropriate strategies for working with students from diverse cultural backgrounds. Teachers who employ such skills *create* classroom communities where diverse students respect and support one another. Differences are discussed and valued, and cultural conflicts are viewed as opportunities for learning. All children will benefit from interacting with children from other cultures. That is how English speakers become more tolerant and learn to value diversity.

Art of Compassion and Kindness

The SEL Department of Sacramento City Unified School District, under the leadership of Mai Xi Lee, coordinated a district-wide event where students from K–12 were invited to submit original creations in the areas of visual and performing arts representing the Art of Compassion in 2017 and the Art of Kindness in 2018. More than 500 students, parents, faculty, and staff, the superintendent and school board, community representatives, and the mayor and city council attended the event each year.

Jasmine Yang   Selena Daniels

Figure 2.8 Artwork from the Art of Compassion Event (Luther Burbank HS, Sacramento)

Pa Chia Yang, Luther Burbank HS   Tina Thao, Luther Burbank HS

Figure 2.9 Artwork from the Art of Compassion Event (Luther Burbank HS, Sacramento)

Showing respect and valuing diversity of language and culture of ELs can be explicitly taught in the classroom but practiced through a number of activities. When teachers value and model social awareness competencies and behaviors they want the students to exhibit, they should also promote activities that target the SEL competencies of respect, empathy, compassion, and kindness. The following was born out of the ridicule and mispronouncing of names.

Eliminating Social Isolation through Relationships

The My Name, My Identity initiative is a collaboration between the Santa Clara County Office of Education (SCCOE) and the National Association for Bilingual Education (NABE). The goal of the "My Name, My Identity" initiative is to build a more inclusive, respectful culture by asking educators and community members to make a pledge honoring students', neighbors', and co-workers' identities by promising to learn how to pronounce the names of international students correctly. In the context of global education, it is important that students feel proud of who they are and have the ability to connect with people from different languages and backgrounds. Names may have deep and important ties to both family history and culture, and making the extra effort to use a person's preferred name and pronounce it correctly is a small step that can create a big impact.

Source: Santa Clara County Office of Education (SCCOE 2021) and National Association for Bilingual Education (NABE)

Figure 2.10 My Name, My Identity

Dr. Yee Wan, Director of Multilingual Education Services for Santa Clara County Office of Education, had the idea for the campaign given her own personal experience of being called the wrong name as a newcomer and EL. She explains the ties between one's name and one's identity and the implications when people do not bother to learn the student's correct name. Mispronouncing a student's name does have an impact on their identity and by mispronouncing a name, it may indicate the teacher or the students are not taking the time to get to know that individual. How does this impact their sense of belonging at school?

"Mispronouncing a student's name essentially renders that student invisible," says Carmen Fariña, former chancellor of New York City Schools, who was an EL and experienced years of teachers mispronouncing and laughing at her last name. A study produced by Kohli and Solórzano (2012), "Teachers Please Learn Our Names! Racial Microaggressions and the K12 Classroom," about the microaggressions and the subtle slights that are painfully obvious and hurtful to the person receiving them, is littered with stories of students who endured shame, anxiety, or embarrassment, and sometimes a mix of all three, when their names were called in class.

Another student-based initiative to promote kindness within the classroom and throughout the school is No One Eats Alone. Many students new to a school or to the country experience social isolation, loneliness, and bullying that can lead to self-harm and community violence. Studies indicate that the negative impacts of social isolation include increased rates of academic failure and truancy, and increased risk of adverse medical outcomes, including poor cardiovascular health, obesity, and substance abuse. Students have shown that, given the tools, they will stand up for others as empathetic and caring activists, not passive bystanders.

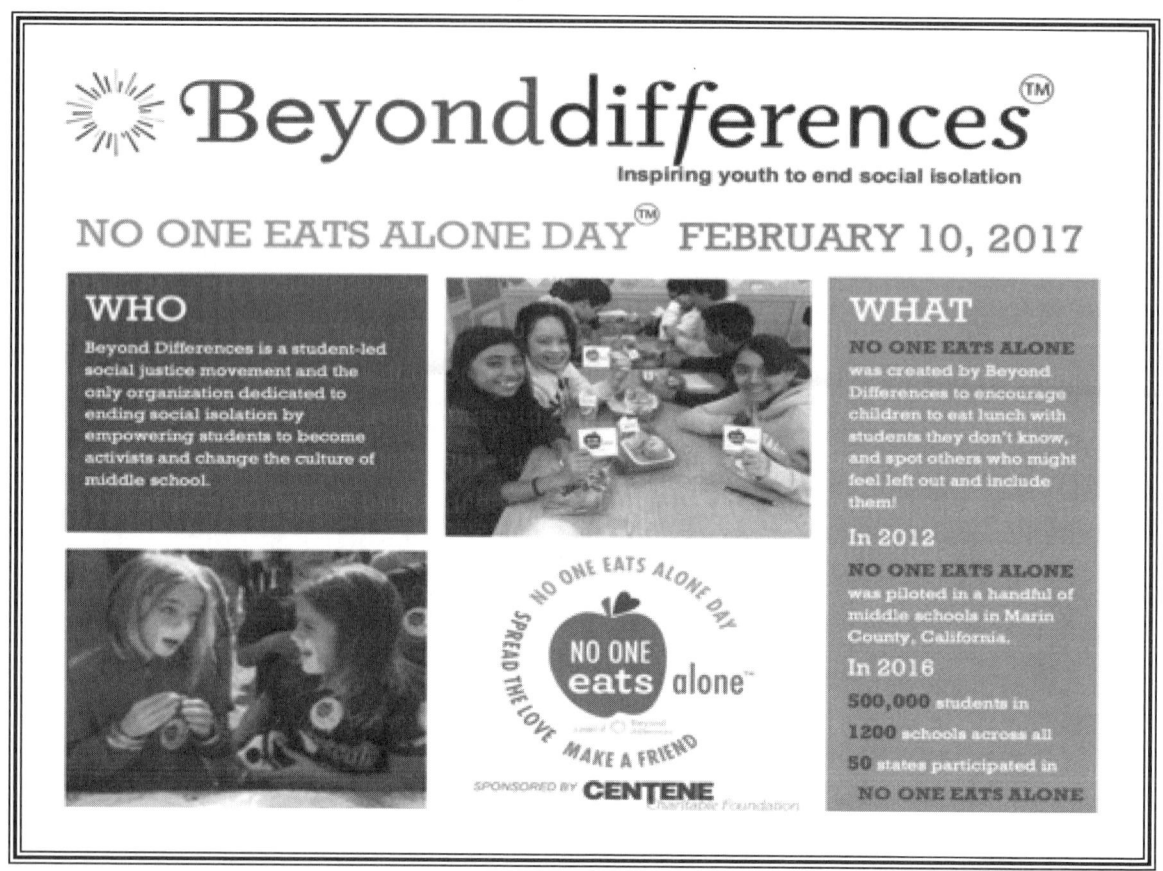

Figure 2.11 No One Eats Alone Day (Beyond Differences 2021)

No One Eats Alone™ is one such program that is a positive prevention initiative that works to prevent bullying before it starts by teaching students to lead the movement to change the culture of a school. No One Eats Alone was created by Beyond Differences to encourage children to eat lunch with students they do not know, and spot others who might feel left out and include them. This is intended to make all kids feel included, valued, and accepted by their peers where social inclusion is the new reality.

This is a great opportunity to have students get to know ELs and LTELs and introduce them to other friends. This is a great way for ELs to learn English in a social context, feel accepted, and become motivated to participate in school-related activities as well as to eliminate social isolation, which often leads to bullying and violence. No One Eats Alone is a powerful incentive for students to become familiar with other language groups and cultures and learn how to correctly pronounce names and practice empathy, compassion, and kindness.

The Great Kindness Challenge (GKC) is another very successful student-led initiative that allows students to further develop their SEL skills while having a positive impact on ELs and newcomers. Teaching students to understand and practice kindness is very different than teaching math, literacy, or science. Kindness and empathy have historically been explicitly taught in PreK but there is an increasing awareness that middle and high school students also need to have a continued conversation concerning kindness, empathy, and other components of social and emotional learning.

This means that secondary teachers, school counselors, and district leaders are all actively searching for ways to teach kindness and empathy, and looking for research to better understand the science behind these competencies. ELs and LTELs are in urgent need of being accepted, embraced, and supported by their English-speaking peers. Given proper guidance, this approach can help English-speaking students volunteer to reach out to their struggling peers and make the success of LTELs a community responsibility. With the current emphasis on social distancing and remote learning, the GKC has not only gone global but is in the process of developing SEL mini lessons and Virtual Classroom Edition checklist, videos, and visuals that can be shared virtually.

Figure 2.12 The Great Kindness Challenge (2021)

Relationship Skills *are the ability to establish and maintain healthy and rewarding relationships with diverse individuals and groups, which includes communicating clearly, listening actively, cooperating, resisting inappropriate social pressure, negotiating conflict constructively, and seeking help when needed.*

Figure 2.13 Definition of relationship skills

It is always best when teachers build relationships with their students but just as important that they become skilled in establishing and maintaining positive student-to-student relationships. Traditionally, the focus on building student-to-student relationships has received more attention at the elementary level because of the nature of self-contained classrooms and the need to be more nurturing with the young lives—whereas learning at the secondary level is generally viewed as teacher centered, traditional seating in rows, competitive, independent seatwork, rote memorization, and a tightly controlled classroom environment.

However, as new students take their seats virtually and in the classroom at all levels, teachers are now faced with the daunting task of creating a sense of community and belonging in order to motivate students to want to learn. In many respects, this is a new skill set that most educators are not familiar with. These skills were not taught to new teachers at the graduate level and veteran teachers have no experience to draw on in order to mentor new teachers on how to create a learning community under circumstances that much more restrictive and isolating than before the pandemic. Administrators are struggling to develop new policies and procedures that would hold teachers accountable for their teaching effectiveness. The consequences of failing to make this transition quickly and effectively has already resulted in students mentally checking out, making it even more difficult to re-engage them in the learning process.

Virtual community building strategies are desperately needed and should be a priority along with alternative approaches to teaching the content. Accomplishing this in mixed learning environments has already proven to be a challenge. This is an entirely new skill set that very few educators have any experience with. For example, the SEL practice of conducting community circles and morning meetings to facilitate students getting to know one another, setting norms of collaboration, and establishing shared agreements now has to be done virtually or socially distanced in the classroom. Some of the benefits of conducting morning meetings and community circles include

1. encourages cooperation and inclusion
2. builds community and creates a climate of trust
3. improves students' reading, writing, listening, and speaking skills
4. gives students daily practice in respectful communication

In addition, teachers need to slow down, learn how to reestablish relationships on a different level, and not be so anxious to get to teaching the traditional curriculum. Parental support is critical

Competency: Relationship Skills

Understanding what others are feeling; being able to take their perspective;
appreciating and interacting positively with diverse groups.

Standard	Indicator	Activities
4A—Interact and communicate clearly, positively, and effectively with others to resolve conflict.	Individual demonstrates the ability to communicate positively using effective language.	Design group activities that take multiple talents. Discuss how the team could best work together by using one another's strengths.
	Individual uses communication and social skills to positively interact with others.	Hold class meetings designed to build class unity and empowerment.
4B—Establish and maintain positive and healthy relationships with diverse groups and individuals.	Individual uses a range of communication skills to interact effectively with individuals of diverse backgrounds, abilities, languages, and lifestyles.	Given a real-life scenario, students design the "teams" they would assemble to best meet the need given—and explain why and how that group would meet the need.
	Individual demonstrates ability to collaborate with others to cultivate constructive relationships with individuals.	In groups, students write radio broadcasts advertising the importance of constructive relationships.
	Individual can read social cues and respond appropriately.	Students draw a fence and label it with behaviors that fit within and without their personal boundaries.
4C—Demonstrate the ability to prevent, manage, and resolve interpersonal conflicts in constructive ways.	Individual demonstrates the skills to respectfully engage in, prevent, and resolve interpersonal conflicts in various contexts.	Students work in pairs using puppets to identify conflicts and show responses. Use class discussion to determine whether the conflict needs an adult helper.
	Practice strategies for maintaining positive relationships (for example, pursue shared interests and activities, spend time together, give and receive help, practice forgiveness).	Students draw a web of support. Next to each person's name on the web, write one strategy they could use to maintain or activate that friendship or support.

Source: SEL standards and indicators are adopted from the Anchorage School District,
Oakland Unified School District PreK–Adult Social and Emotional Learning Standards and El Paso Learning Standards.

Table 2.4 SEL standards and competencies for Relationship Skills

ELs at all levels of language proficiency benefit from cooperative learning activities because they are an excellent strategy to facilitate relationship building. If done properly, cooperative learning activities allow LTELs to work in small group settings, have multiple opportunities to use language, make mistakes and take risks, and learn from peers who are at various academic and language ability levels. What better way to explicitly teach, model, and reinforce empathy with English speakers who will be working cooperatively with ELs than through cooperative learning strategies. Teaching social skills and relationship building should be a high priority prior to engaging in cooperative learning activities. This could be done through a process of establishing shared agreements, morning meetings, and community circles. These are all precursors to preparing students to be able to participate effectively and intentionally practice SEL competencies while participating in cooperative learning activities.

Cooperative learning strategies that are used school wide can achieve full student participation at all grade levels, provide practice time for SEL competencies and academic content integration, allow students to exchange ideas, promote discourse and empathic listening skills and engagement in academic dialog to express, summarize, and synthesize information while facilitating team and individual accountability. SEL skills and competencies that are practiced during cooperative learning activities allow LTELs to practice academic integration with language and literacy in all core content areas.

Incorporating cooperative learning strategies that emphasize SEL competencies in the content areas allows teachers to check ELs' understanding of the specific competency to be practiced, assess what skills need to be retaught, and monitor the degree of their social interaction with other students. This is a sure way to help LTELs build social confidence and gives them an incentive to ask for help without fear of humiliation or embarrassment. Cooperative learning practices have the potential to accelerate academic learning for LTELs, enhance student-centered learning environments, and facilitate the differentiation of instruction. We will share some cooperative learning strategies that relate to vocabulary, reading, and writing instruction in later chapters.

Most notably, cooperative learning strategies can provide maximum opportunities for ELs to practice social and academic language in safe and supportive environments, resulting in students becoming more academically productive, better behaved, and less likely to drop out. Cooperative learning strategies are most effective when

- learning norms, protocols, and SEL competencies are established with students for what is expected of them during each activity
- students are given tasks, not roles, for their performance during each lesson
- strategies for cooperative learning, classroom management, and reinforcement of SEL competencies go hand in hand

You will see these strategies throughout the chapters.

There are a number of cooperative learning strategies that have proven to be useful when working with LTELs, including

- team building/class building
- clearly defining cooperative teams and norms of collaboration
- pair-share and partner reading
- triads and mixed groupings
- round robin—variations
- roundtable literacy activities

> ***Responsible Decision Making*** *is the ability to make constructive choices about personal behavior, social interactions, and school, which includes considering ethical standards, safety concerns, social norms, the consequences of various actions, and the well-being of self and others. Responsible decisions reflect concern for one's well-being as well as the well-being of others.*

Figure 2.14 Definition of responsible decision-making

There are many compelling reasons why Responsible Decision Making on the part of educators is one of the most critical SEL competency when it comes to the plight of LTELs. This competency needs to be strengthened and not be considered optional, especially in light of the fact that LTELs have suffered from ridicule, social segregation, low expectations, and discriminatory practices at all levels of the school environment. Here is what LTELs have experienced when it comes to institutional segregation and discriminatory practices.

1. There are no clear and consistent practices of onboarding and welcoming ELs into a new learning environment.
2. Testing and placement practices may be in place, but far too often accurate assessment and past educational history are not taken into consideration when prescribing appropriate placement in classes that might accelerate learning and reclassification, as with Sandra in the case study in chapter one.
3 Parents' home language, culture, and economic status are not taken into consideration when communicating about school requirements, procedures, policies, homework, parent meetings, discipline, career planning, and academic requirements for promotion and graduation.

4   Administrators, teachers, and other adults in the schools often lack adequate training in SEL competencies and skills to facilitate the social integration of ELs and LTELs in the classroom, in extracurricular activities, and with English-dominant students.

5   Even if SEL has been implemented by a school or school district and an evidence-based program has been adopted, the language of instruction is almost always in English, resulting in ELs being excluded from another important tier of academic learning and social integration.

6   Teachers may be caring, welcoming, and wanting their students to be successful, but the benefits to LTELs of fully and effectively implementing instructional practices such as cooperative learning, classroom discussions, balanced instruction, and competence building are not fully understood or appreciated.

7   LTELs are far too often not provided meaningful and challenging assignments and their teachers sometimes do not believe that they can complete rigorous work, as was the case with Sandra in the case study in chapter one.

By using positive energy and collective wisdom to change and redefine the way things used to be we can now make more responsible decisions to better prepare all students to help create a brighter future. It is important that we reflect on the past and identify what needed to be learned but most importantly that we take the initiative in making decisions that make education better for all students, including ELs.

In order to move forward, we need to reflect on data that best describes the consequences of the current inequitable educational system that has failed to serve the needs of ELs and LTELs (Olsen 2010).

---

1. *A total of 75 percent to 80 percent of ELs nationwide are LTELs.*

2. *They have been in US schools since K–1 or at least six years and labeled Limited English Proficient (LEP) and are typically second- or even third-generation citizens.*

3. *Sometimes they are hiding under other labels (expanding, bridging, expanding or novice, intermediate, initial fluent English proficient).*

Figure 2.15 Data on ELs and LTELs

If the practices of the past did not work for 75 percent of the students, will we be able to do anything differently now that we are facing the challenge to make it work for our LTELs who are even more negatively impacted by the pandemic than most other populations? In the past, the LTEL achievement gaps were created by years of ineffective language, literacy, and content instruction in their first and second language. Here are past and current deficiencies in the exciting instructional practices that need to be acknowledged and addressed before any progress for LTELs can be made.

1. Reading skills were superficial at best.

2. Academic writing was yet to be developed.

3. Low sense of self-efficacy.

4. In great need of social-emotional understanding by educators.

Competency: Responsible Decision Making

Understanding what others are feeling; being able to take their perspective; appreciating and interacting positively with diverse groups.

Standard	Indicator	Activities
5A—Make constructive and respectful choices that consider the well-being of self and others, especially ELs.	Individual considers the well-being of self and others when making decisions.	In small groups have teams determine strategies they could use to manage various situations. Act them out and evaluate their usefulness.
	Individual considers ethical and societal factors in making decisions.	Play a game where the rules are unfair in some way. Discuss students' behaviors and feelings in the midst of the game.
5B—Behave responsibly in personal, professional, and community contexts.	Individual understands and demonstrates personal responsibility.	Students write their own "self-help" manuals to show conflict-resolution skills. Include at least one true story where another response would have been more beneficial.
	Individual demonstrates integrity by being honest and behaving ethically in all situations.	Play "Telephone" and then discuss how messages can so easily get misconstrued when someone does not listen or talk carefully.
5C—Problem-solve effectively while being respectful of people similar to and different from oneself.	Individual applies problem-solving skills while being respectful of people similar to and different from themselves in a variety of situations.	Hold class debates over a particular issue that must end in a win–win for the class to be successful.
	Individual applies problem-solving skills to responsibly address daily academic and social situations.	Have peer mediators discuss the steps of conflict resolution in a class presentation.

Source: SEL standards and indicators are adopted from the Anchorage School District, Oakland Unified School District PreK–Adult Social and Emotional Learning Standards and El Paso Learning Standards

Table 2.5 SEL standards and competencies for Responsible Decision Making

New Decisions about Language and Literacy for LTEL

In many ways LTELs have suffered from the "reading wars" that have confused teachers for so many years. Consider the meaning of Responsible Decision Making in the context of the instructional practices listed below. What have your LTELs experienced when it came to reading instruction?

1. *Too much phonics?* They can decode fairly well; their fluency sounds quite nice. Then, you ask them what they read, and they cannot tell you.
2. *Too much whole language?* They love the stories you read and can talk about character traits and story details. However, they cannot read these stories by themselves.
3. *Too much unbalanced literacy?* LTELs have listening, speaking, reading, writing, and content comprehension gaps due to unaligned, inappropriate, and poorly implemented literacy programs.
4. *Too much sheltering?* LTELs were always reading books "at their level" and never taught how to read closely or "muddle through a text" after being taught key vocabulary and sentence features that will enable comprehension and tenacity as they read.
5. *Not enough reading comprehension instruction?* Reading in the areas of science, math, and social studies is different from reading in language arts or ESL classrooms. The text structures, text features, and subject-specific vocabulary vary considerably. Unless science, math, and social studies teachers point these out, LTEL and other striving readers cannot delve deeper into comprehension.

Here are a few ways that teachers can begin to integrate SEL with academics. For example, vocabulary terms for the pandemic, politics, and social unrest have shifted to take on new meanings; that is, they have become more polysemous (words with multiple meanings). One illustration would be the word "distance," "distancing," and "demonstrate." New concepts and meanings are also emerging from word clusters such as coronavirus, COVID-19, social separation, physical distancing, food insecurity, pandemic flare ups, Stay-At-Home Order, Black Lives Matter, social justice, organized anarchists, synchronous and asynchronous learning, and economic downturn. From an SEL context, words such as "anxiety," "stress," "depression," "trauma," "quarantine," "empathy," and "compassion" have become more commonly used and experienced at all levels of society and globally. Examples such as these take on new meanings for many students but more so for ELs and LTELs. Language is rapidly shifting, just as our old ways of thinking, believing, and behaving are shifting.

The following words and definitions will be used for the rapidly changing learning contexts even though the precise definitions are still emerging. As is often the case in English, more usage will determine more precision and ultimately keep the preferred nomenclature.

- **Asynchronous:** Teaching/Learning in which students can choose when to engage in a particular experience. One example would be pre-recorded videos that students can watch at any time, or readings and assignments that students can complete at any time. Self-paced teaching/learning is a synonym for Asynchronous Teaching/Learning.
- **Synchronous:** Teaching/Learning that includes all participants (teacher and students) engaging in the experience at the same time. Examples include face-to-face teaching and live, facilitated virtual courses.
- **Virtual:** Teaching/Learning that takes place via the Internet. Could be synchronous or asynchronous.
- **Distance:** Teaching/Learning that takes place when the teacher and the student are geographically separated. Could be virtual (via the Internet), but it does not have to be. Teaching/Learning through books and paper packets that are mailed back and forth between teacher and student, for example, would be distance learning.
- **Remote:** Synonymous with distance learning/teaching.
- **Hybrid:** Teaching/Learning that uses a blend of two things: face-to-face experiences in a classroom, and virtual learning via the Internet. The virtual learning component could be synchronous or asynchronous.
- **Blended:** This can be synonymous with hybrid learning/teaching, but some people make a distinction between hybrid teaching/learning and blended teaching/learning based on how the two types of teaching/learning are divided. If all students engage in face-to-face learning at one time and virtual learning at another time, this is more likely to be called blended teaching/learning. If all students are learning at the same time, but some are face-to-face with the teacher while others are interacting virtually, that is more likely to be called hybrid teaching/learning. Like all language, though, these terms are sure to change over time as teachers and students find more reasons to talk about the different ways they interact.

Transitioning to the New Way of Schooling

Many enlightened schools opted for two ways of reaching out to their ELs: virtual, online (i.e., email), and telephone but also by delivering packets with the weekly lessons and/or EL guides to better understand the virtual instruction. They recognize the following research findings.

- Vocabulary knowledge correlates with reading comprehension and LTELs need to be mastering 3,000—5,000 words per year in order to comprehend.
- With ample vocabulary, reading comprehension skills will begin to correlate with procedural (metacognitive) and content knowledge.
- The more LTELs read expository text, the better they write and the more content they master.
- As we know, content knowledge correlates with academic success (Zacarian, Calderón, and Gottlieb 2021).

Tim Shanahan (2020) states the importance of reading in a recent blog that is relevant not only for LTEL but for all students who may be striving to read at grade level.

> But if we're serious about higher reading achievement—about breaking out of the unremitting mediocrity that sustains current reading levels but never improves them, that keeps children who live in poverty, Black children, immigrant children, and children with disabilities far below the levels of literacy they'll need to gain the full the benefits of our society—then we must change what we are doing. (Shanahan 2020)

Long-Term ELs are not just the ESL/ELD teacher's responsibility anymore—*it's the entire school's responsibility*. Language and literacy have to be embedded in all core content classrooms. LTELs need to engage in cognitively challenging language, literacy, and content instruction in all classrooms that are infused with SEL competencies and practices. It is highly recommended that teachers consider starting a transition plan with the following points in mind and actionable year-long goals for the school.

Planning and Implementing the Transition Plan

1. Think equity and support for LTELs and all multicultural learners.
2. Think SEL for LTEL support (for example, addressing stress, trauma, family engagement, peer relationships, and virtual relationships).
3. Address LTEL's academic gaps (for example, curriculum planning, assessing, accelerating academic language, basic reading skills, reading comprehension, academic writing, higher order thinking in all core content areas).
4. Build teacher capacity (for example, teacher wellness, professional development, collegial commitment, and continuous collaboration)
5. Embrace a new strategy for operations (for example, leadership wellness, professional development, vision, mission, planning, school safety, staffing, communications, and iterations when necessary).

These are only a few considerations that must be assessed before specific strategies are implemented and programmatic considerations are adopted that would ultimately address the needs of LTELs. In subsequent chapters, there will be a greater emphasis on language and literacy in an SEL-rich learning environment.

Conclusion

Despite the uncertainty of the current state of global affairs, there is a ray of hope and optimism that not only will we get through this together, but that we will be willing partners in co-creating a better and brighter future that is more inclusive, more compassionate, and affords greater opportunities for ELs and LTELs. We can be hopeful that teachers and administrators will be willing to become more familiar with SEL competencies, strategies, and practices to actively welcome ELs into new learning environments, placing ELs in appropriate classes that accelerate learning, honor and respect parents' home language, culture, and economic status and communicate to them about school events and requirements in a language and tone that they can respond to and understand. We need to be hopeful that administrators, teachers, and other adults in schools receive extensive training in SEL competencies and skills in order to better facilitate the social integration and academic success of ELs and LTELs in core content classrooms. In other words, LTELs need caring and compassionate teachers to use the necessary instructional tools and set high expectations to ensure that LTELs are academically successful and socially integrated so that they are college and career ready.

Personal Reflections and Collegial Discussions

1. Which SEL competencies are needed to enhance the inclusion and success of LTELs?

   _____

   _____

2. How can SEL encourage, instruct, and engage English-dominant students in becoming more culturally aware and culturally responsive to LTELs?

   _____

   _____

3. What SEL strategies can teachers promote to enhance academic achievement for LTELs?

   _____

   _____

4. How can professional development on SEL help adults develop their SEL competencies and sustain them over time?

   _____

   _____

5. Which SEL practices could be implemented in classrooms that would help ELs become more confident in participating in instructional activities?

   _____

   _____

6. In what ways does the implementation of SEL-related activities ultimately benefit LTELs?

   _____

   _____

7. How would you monitor and measure the effectiveness of integrating SEL skills and strategies with teaching academic language to ELs?

   _____

   _____

Chapter 3

Integrating SEL in Instruction

This transition to mixed-learning environments has created a need for redefining teacher–student relationships, student–student relationships, communications, and instructional delivery methods. This change of venue has put a tremendous amount of stress on the teachers, administrators, as well as on policy makers to respond effectively to the drastic change to a more unpredictable and uncertain world. As with the students, teachers are in critical need of support, encouragement, and assistance in redefining norms and protocols for this new reality. Even though there has been a rapid response for the need for equipment, training and policy to address the demands for a safe and effective learning environment, teachers and parents are stretched to the limits emotionally.

How Can SEL Make a Difference?

Most importantly, beginning with a greater focus on social and emotional learning is essential to get students to want to participate in a remote hybrid or face-to-face but socially distanced learning environment. There are many SEL practices, activities, and lessons available that are designed for face-to-face interaction. However, translating those practices into a mixed-learning platform is even more difficult but certainly not impossible. One such approach is utilizing the SEL 3 Signature Practices framework for both the classroom and adults as a foundation to develop strategies and practices to address the current needs of all students (CASEL 2019a). They were developed in response to a greater interest in knowing what SEL looks like in the classroom and in adult interactions. The goal of the SEL Three Signature Practices is to create a safe, inclusive, and caring community of learners where students have equity of voice and where their culture, language, and values are acknowledged, appreciated, and understood. These strategies were designed to help students and adults develop and use SEL skills and competencies in a number of circumstances that would contribute to their success in school, careers, and in life. This chapter will utilize this framework to identify practices and strategies that will assist LTELs to excel in an environment that validates their history, identity, and need for a sense of belonging while promoting the practice of LTELs and ELs partnering with English-speaking students.

The SEL Three Signature Practices are:

- ✔ **Welcoming Routines and Rituals**—setting the tone, activities for inclusion
- ✔ **Engaging Pedagogy and Strategies**—sense making, transitions, brain breaks
- ✔ **Optimistic Closure**—reflections and looking forward

When used consistently, carefully chosen, and facilitated effectively these SEL practices can create conditions for ELs to thrive, especially when used in conjunction with culturally responsive teaching and cooperative learning strategies. They create opportunities for students and adults to further develop and practice the Five Core SEL Competencies from relationship building to academic integration.

Welcoming Routines and Rituals are brief and interactive activities intended to promote activities for inclusion, establishing a safe learning environment for all students to participate and feel noticed, appreciated, and valued.

Figure 3.1 Definition of welcoming routines and rituals

Welcoming routines and rituals should be predictable and a consistent part of a daily routine so that students know what to expect at the beginning of a regular or virtual class meeting. Done properly and in concert with explicit instruction on SEL competencies, welcoming rituals facilitate the interaction and connection of students with one another and affords them multiple opportunities to practice relationship building and social awareness skills. This is a powerful strategy to assist ELs to become more trusting, confident, and motivated to participate in class-related activities without the fear of being embarrassed or shamed.

Intentionally facilitating the interaction between students from diverse backgrounds during the welcoming routines and rituals will not only set the stage for subsequent instructional activities to be more inclusive and caring but will also contribute to creating and sustaining a more equitable learning environment. For ELs and LTELs, who are already facing inequities in education, housing, health, and employment opportunities and even digitally, would flourish in an equity-centered learning environment.

The following are the three essential elements of an equitable learning and working environment as defined in the *SEL 3 Signature Practices Playbook* (2019, p. 7).

1. Equity of voice: All participants are encouraged to speak and are respectfully heard.
2. Inclusion: All degrees of participation are welcomed and acknowledged.

3. Collectivism: All engage in and contribute to a "for the good of the group" experience.

Below are additional activities that could be used during welcoming routines and rituals that would be beneficial to ELs and LTELs and can be done during class meetings and community circles or virtually. These are but a few ideas that could serve as attentions getters and community

Welcoming Routines and Rituals: Attention getters and community builders		
1. Check-ins	12. Charades	21. Bring Something to the Camera
2. Mood Meter	13. Dress-up games	22. Pictionary or Draw and Guess using a whiteboard app
3. My Name, My Identity	14. Simon Says	
4. Mindfulness exercises	15. What's This Sound?	23. Correct My Lies
5. Four Corners*	16. Virtual Bingo using the language in the content	24. Describe and Draw games
6. Greeting Frenzy*	17. What Do I Have in My Hand?	25. Storytelling game using the words "fortunately" and "unfortunately"
7. Name and Motion*	18. Show and Tell	
8. One, Two, Three, Clap!*	19. Chants and songs	26. Community Building activities
9. Mix and Mingle*	20. Memory games	
10 Synectics*		
11. What's New? *		

Source: Adapted from *SEL 3 Signature Practices Playbook*, 2019.

Table 3.1 Welcoming Routines and Rituals

Shared Agreements and Norms of Virtual Collaboration

Foundational to well-designed and motivating welcoming rituals are the development, practice, and reinforcement of Shared Agreements and Norms of Virtual Collaboration that integrate and promote the 5 Core SEL Competencies. Class norms and agreements need to be renewed with each new class and even more so now in the context of a virtual setting. Of added value and most impactful for ELs and LTELs is embedding SEL competencies such as relationship building, valuing diversity, empathy, compassion, respect, and responsible decision-making.

Ideally, any shared agreements and norms should be defined and agreed to collaboratively during community circles or morning meetings. Having students collaboratively establish and commit to adhering to shared agreements and class norms would greatly benefit ELs and LTELs because the process would afford them the opportunity to voice their opinions, feel that their ideas and contributions are valued and appreciated while practicing language in a social context. These are collaboratively developed and mutually accepted agreements and are essential to making the experience of welcoming rituals meaningful, secure, rewarding, and academically beneficial for ELs.

This process of co-creating agreements further promotes the goal of LTELs being able to see and hear their English-speaking peers model native level language proficiency while actively participating in a learning environment that values diversity, shows empathy toward students who are learning English, and demonstrates an ability to understand and accept perspectives that are different from theirs.

Shared agreements could be as simple as formal greetings, expressions of appreciation, empathic listening practices, encouraging others, offering help when needed, and respecting differences of opinions.

Shared Agreements

1. Beginning on time	8. Active listening	15. Working cooperatively
2. Actively participating	9. Willingness to explore new ideas with an open mind	16. Use communication and social skills to interact effectively with others
3. Staying engaged	10. Embrace new approaches to learning	17. Resolve conflicts in constructive and restorative ways
4. Greeting each other warmly	11. Ping Pong	
5. Valuing student voice	12. Round Table Summaries	18. Communicate your thoughts and feelings
6. Recognizing the feelings and perspectives of others	13. Give Me Five	
7. Thanking each other after sharing ideas	14. Give and receive help	

Table 3.2 Shared Agreements

Even though these agreements are pre-pandemic, they are just as applicable to the current mixed-learning environments. The goal is not just to have agreements as an end in itself, but to make them more meaningful by explicitly teaching, modeling, and reinforcing them in every social and academic interaction.

In addition to shared agreements, norms of collaboration are just as important from both the technical or virtual perspective as well as with in-person instruction. They should be practiced with any kind of learning platform. Since these are both practical and of a more technical nature, they need not be developed collaboratively but must be clearly understood and non-negotiable. They are: Rename, Be Present, Empathic Listening, Equal Time, Reflections and Debrief.

Rename

Participants in any platform should always be asked to make sure that their full name is visible on the screen or even to wear name tags at the beginning of the year. This should be the expectation rather than the exception for all gatherings and considered an essential ingredient for students to build relationships and to be more socially aware. As is the general practice in classrooms, mostly at the secondary level, students are not usually encouraged to get to know each other by name, much less wear name tags. This has worked against ELs getting to know their peers by name and has denied English-speaking students the opportunity to see ELs' names in writing and to practice pronouncing their names. This oversight has contributed to the isolation and loneliness that students in general experience in traditional secondary classrooms and most notably a barrier for ELs who want to make friends, belong, and feel accepted and respected.

The My Name, My Identity initiative (SCCOE 2016) has contributed to the rapid building of relationships and bonding between students, resulting in students reaching out to one another in a show of support, empathy, and inclusion. As a result, ELs have reported being invited to participate in both class and out-of-class activities by their English-speaking peers, thus building their self-esteem and self-confidence. This is why the practice of renaming should be one of the Gold Standards in both the in-person and virtual worlds. It will make communications much more effective for students when they participate in small group gatherings, such as check-ins, project-based activities, partner reading, and ping-ponging during vocabulary-building activities.

Be Present

The practice of Being Present is posing a serious challenge for both students and teachers in face-to-face and virtual settings. This is a practice and discipline that deserves special attention because it will contribute to adults and students becoming more self-aware and able to manage emotions more effectively. Due to the instantaneous access to information, resources, and social media through technology, students have become obsessed with multitasking, resulting in them becoming easily distracted and having very short attention spans except when the objects of attention are entertaining, fast paced, or full of suspense. Teachers are rapidly discovering that students have an even shorter attention span during instructional times on the screen compared to the classroom. This has forced teachers to craft their lessons into shorter soundbites, integrate more visuals and soundtracks, facilitate more student-to-student interactions, and retire the traditional command and control style of teaching.

Exacerbating the problem of getting students to participate in regularly scheduled distance learning sessions are the lack of connectivity, scarcity of equipment, and the lack of adult supervision. In addition, teachers are being confronted with the added challenge of students not having structured schedules and routines for months coupled with inadequate and irregular sleeping and eating habits. Even when on the screen, students are finding other things to do while appearing to be listening to teacher talk.

The art and discipline of Being Present should not be taken for granted but must be intentionally and explicitly taught and practiced as an important SEL competency. One option to taming the emotions and focusing the mind are mindfulness practices, which have found their way into classrooms across the country with impressive results. Teachers are finding that mindfulness practices can even be used as part of a welcoming ritual to help students get focused and to be more attentive and engaging during the lesson. A quick body scan, five finger breathing exercises, or guided meditation practices are effective exercises that teachers can use to get students to be present, to refocus their attention, and to use as a brain break. Just as teachers want students to be present, teachers also need to be present and attuned to student needs rather than rushing to "cover the content."

Empathic Listening

Explicitly teaching empathy and what it looks like would help students discover that empathic listening has some unique traits, skill sets, and benefits that will greatly contribute to their own personal growth and development while appreciating the stories, thoughts, and dreams of their peers. Empathy comes under the Social Skills SEL framework and empathic listening should be considered a priority for adults and students. Empathic listening can be considered more of an art form rather than a discipline. Students would find it beneficial if teachers first modeled the characteristics of effective listening skills and then arrange breakout rooms so as to give students opportunities to practice empathic listening skills with their peers.

Developing empathic listening skills would greatly contribute to prevention and resolving of problems, enhance cooperation, and make the time that students have collaborating with one another more valuable, engaging, and productive rather than being dreaded, stressful, or feared. For LTELs, the more their peers practice empathic listening skills with them the more LTELs will be willing to share their stories and feel proud of their language, heritage, and culture.

Equal Time

Nothing is more valuable for students than to have the opportunity to be heard. The benefits of giving students equal time to participate and share is dependent on the degree to which students and adults have established positive relationships, have the ability to be present, and possess the skills of empathic listening. Equal time is steeped in the practice of equity, culturally responsive teaching, restorative practices, and responsible decision-making.

ELs and LTELs need equal time to practice language, to tell their story, to be noticed, and to practice their newly acquired social and language skills learned from explicit instructional practices that facilitate positive interactions with English-dominant peers. With the added goal of having 100 percent student participation, classroom structures and virtual breakouts need to be designed so that students work in dyads, triads, or quads with the understanding that they will give one another equal time to explore the use of language, express thoughts about an issue, respond to a prompt, share observations of a video, and even hear the personal stories of others. Equal time means equal time and where adults make the responsible decision to intentionally facilitate this practice, students will thrive.

As with cooperative learning strategies discussed later in this chapter, students should have specific roles to ensure that the time ELs have to share in breakout rooms is guarded, protected, and honored by the other students involved. Not only should there be a timekeeper to keep everyone on track, but a process guide should be assigned to ensure that the highest levels of respect, courtesy, and SEL skills are practiced and upheld. Any time a group or breakout room activity is planned then clear directions, guiding prompts, review of the norms and shared agreements to be practiced, and clarity on the allocated time should be explicitly taught, reinforced, and monitored during the activity. There should be no ambiguity and compromise on the expectation that all students practice SEL competencies and have equal time.

Once the skill of empathic listening coupled with the practice of respecting equal time have been solidified with students, check-ins can be a great way to have students interact and share stories, reflect on feelings, and turn to one another for support, advice, and encouragement. Doing check-ins face-to-face can be as simple as turning to your neighbor or pair sharing with a Clock Buddy or Academic Vocabulary Buddy (to be discussed in the next section).

Check-In

- *Breakout Rooms or groups of four people*
- *Introduce yourselves and birthday*
- *Go in order of birthday—January on*

- *What's going well for you right now*
- *Name one current challenge, fear, or growth opportunity*
- *Reflections as a group*

Figure 3.2 Check-ins for interaction

Virtually, this can be easily facilitated when a breakout room function is available. Above is an example of instructions to be posted on a screen or entered in a Chat Box for a Welcoming Ritual breakout activity for students in upper elementary to high school.

Reflections/Debrief

Carving out time for students to make meaning of their learning enhances comprehension, facilitates social and idea networking, encourages students to look for commonalities and differences in their thinking, and allows ELs and LTELs to practice targeted vocabulary and grammar. The practice of "reflecting" is more about processing experiences and transferring learning to real-life and future learning, whereas "debriefing" may seem more like describing the sequence of events and the dynamics involved. Both are important components of this exercise.

This practice also helps students move to a deeper level of conversation. Allowing students to process and share what they have learned permits teachers to gain a deeper understanding of the student's knowledge, experience, level of comprehension, and interest in the topic. This could be conducted through the Chat Box or doing a Speak Out activity. The Chat Box is an excellent tool to get the majority of students to provide quick answers, making their thoughts visible to everyone. This is one of the great advantages of distance learning: instantaneous responses that can viewed and saved. In addition, the Speak Out activity is also very engaging. It begins by the teacher asking someone who has made an entry in the Chat Box to further explain their response. When that person finishes, then they in turn select the next person to share out. This can also be done in in-person classrooms.

- *What's going well for you right now?*
- *What is your current challenge, fear, or growth opportunity right now?*

Figure 3.3 Chat Box: Speak Out

Depending on the size of the group, this Speak Out activity can be done with three to five students. Encourage students to select LTELs as much as possible. The students have the option to "pass" if they are not comfortable or not prepared to share out. During this reflection/debriefing activity, ELs and LTELs may need sentence starters that would give them tools to participate more fully. In face-to-face instruction, the use of Table Tents with examples for accountable talk and text-based discussions exercises are great helpers for students to get started when it is their turn to speak. Virtually, these examples should be sent to the students, posted on the screen, entered in the Chat Box, and even sent as a broadcast when students are in breakout rooms. This activity should also be included among resources to be used in Optimistic Closures.

Here are a few examples of sentence starters that would give ELs tools to help them increase their participation in class activities and reflections.

Text-Based Discussions	Accountable Talk: Agreement	Accountable Talk: Disagreement
This is about . . . I think this is about . . . I liked the . . . I learned a new word . . . I liked the part where . . . I think this means . . . I don't understand this part . . . That character reminds me of . . . That part reminds me of . . .	I agree . . . I agree, however, I would like to add . . . I want to echo . . . I concur . . . Moreover, . . . Furthermore, . . . Based on . . ., I . . . In addition, . . .	I disagree . . . I respectfully disagree . . . I disagree due to . . . However, the author states . . . On the other hand, . . . However, in the text, . . .

Source: Calderón 2018.

Table 3.2 Shared Agreements

Engaging Pedagogy and Strategies *are practices that are carefully integrated into academics so as to foster relationships, collaboration, empowerment, and smooth transitions. They provide students with opportunities for sense-making and "brain breaks."*

Figure 3.4 Engaging pedagogy and strategies

Practicing Welcoming Routines and Rituals on a regular basis is an excellent way to prepare ELs and LTELs to participate in more meaningful, engaging, and collaborative academic work with their peers. Repeated practice and reinforcement of SEL skills, Shared Agreements and Norms of Virtual Collaboration help students internalize the knowledge, behaviors, skills, and values that are essential for LTELs to further practice English, develop social skills, and experience success both individually and collectively.

When teachers are well grounded in SEL skills and more knowledgeable of specific SEL competencies and standards, they are better able to select and integrate appropriate SEL instructional practices with academic content. Some of these practices include inquiry-based prompts, turn and talk, and cooperative learning activities. This section includes several concrete examples on how SEL competencies and engaging pedagogy can be integrated into the teaching of language and literacy in a way that will be most beneficial for LTELs.

Explicitly teaching SEL competencies and intentionally integrating them into language and literacy instruction can help students be more confident in their academic abilities while being more self-aware of their feelings toward working with their peers from different backgrounds. This ultimately would have the effect of intentionally fostering and sustaining positive relationships between students, broadening their abilities to listen empathically, and being more inclusive. The following table illustrates the difference between traditional instructional practices and those that promote SEL, autonomy, empowerment, belonging, and feelings of self-confidence. LTELs are often stuck in ESL coursework that is primarily independent seatwork, individualized/personalized computer work, rote memorization, and teacher-directed grammar lessons.

In the table below the 'Less' column represents practices more common at the secondary level whereas the 'More' column are practices that are appropriate for all grade levels.

Instructional Practices that Promote SEL and Academic Achievement	
Less	**More**
Teacher lecture	Inquiry/Project-based learning
Disconnected subject areas	Integrated learning
Competition	Cooperation
Rote learning	Critical thinking and problem solving
Independent seatwork	Collaborative structures
Teacher-directed	Student-centered

Table 3.4 Instructional practices that promote SEL

Below are a number of Brain Breaks and Transition Techniques that help with "anchoring learning, regaining focus, enhancing creativity" that are emotionally engaging and will help LTELs better make sense of the material presented.

Brain Breaks and Transition Techniques		
1. Attention Signal	7. Gallery Walk	12. Give One, Get One, Move On
2. Card Sorts	8. Jigsaw	13. Meet in the Middle (Brain Break)
3. Clock Partners	9. Maître d'	14. Mindful Minute (Brain Break)
4. Engaging with Data	10. Pass It On	15. Team Quiz Hustle (Brain Break)
5. Fishbowl	11. Save the Last Word	

Source: *The SEL 3 Signature Practices Playbook* (pp. 20–35)

Table 3.5 Brain Breaks and Transition Techniques

Grouping Strategies

Added to the list of emotionally painful and demoralizing experiences that LTELs have to endure is the feeling of being left out of class-related activities because no one wants to pair with them except members of their own language group. When asked, LTELs are quick to say that their biggest desire is to be able to "make friends" but that they "don't know how" and that teachers do not help them. The common practice of allowing students to practice self-select seating and self-select pairing for class-related activities has the unintended consequences of further segregating students even within the classroom.

Specific tools are needed to intentionally and strategically pair students to "help them" further develop positive relationships, enhance learning, and increase opportunities for students to learn from one another and about one another. Clock Buddies or Clock Partners and Academic Vocabulary Buddies (AVB) are tools that address the social and emotional needs of all students to break through those artificial barriers. Although they differ slightly in their focus, they both follow the same concept of allowing students to select a partner for an "appointment" to discuss, reflect, practice, and engage in content-related activities.

In allowing students to seek out buddies, certain parameters need to be set and behaviors reinforced in order for ELs and LTELs to reap the maximum benefit from this activity; otherwise, students will naturally resegregate themselves. Virtually, the teacher has the option to manually place students in breakout rooms or grouping clusters. This must be done with great care and with the intention to reinforce the class norms, shared agreements, and explicitly taught SEL competencies. Once these initial parameters have been set, the next steps for signing up a buddy for both tools are similar.

1. *Actively practice Shared Agreements and SEL skills such as introducing themselves when finding a new partner, shaking hands, and stating that they are looking forward to meeting with them when that time slot or vocabulary word is announced.*
2. *Seek out someone who they have not had an opportunity to partner with.*
3. *Seek out someone who comes from a language group, culture, gender identity, and race different from your own.*

Source: Calderón 2007

Figure 3.5 Parameters for inclusive pairing strategies

1. *Students have a copy of either Clock Buddy or AVB handout.*
2. *Make sure that they write their name at the top.*
3. *Have participants stand up, and with their papers and something to write with, move quietly around the room until a signal is given for them to find a partner who is nearby. Practice greeting skills.*
4. *Add each other's names on the first available line or box as if setting an appointment.*
5. *Proceed with the process of mixing, stopping, and finding a new partner until all slots are filled with a name of a person with whom they will partner with when the item or time is called.*
6. *Once all lines are signed participants return to their seats.*
7. *Refer to the Clock Buddy or AVB sheets when announcing one of the times or words that will prompt them to get up and meet with their partner for this activity. Depending on the nature of the pairing exercise, they should be given the option to select a meeting place, whether in their seats, on the floor, or standing up.*

Source: Calderón 2007

Figure 3.6 Parameters for inclusive pairing strategies

Academic Vocabulary Buddies

Your Name: _____

Directions: Write the name of a <u>different</u> person in each space to the right. Then add your name on your partner's paper for the same row.

1	**Moreover**	
2	**Over the course of**	
3	**Trunk**	
4	**Effect**	
5	**Initially**	
6	**Processing**	

Source: Calderón 2007

Figure 3.7 Academic Vocabulary Buddies

Academic Vocabulary Buddies is slightly different from Clock Buddies in that it has a greater focus on building vocabulary. Instead of fixed time slots, as with the Clock Buddies handout, the AVB allows the teacher the option to list the vocabulary for the day or week from any subject area as the pairing prompt. This selection of words should be based on vocabulary that is extracted or parsed directly from the content to be covered, to be used during the pairing activities, embedded in the reading and writing exercises, and to be practiced in discourse and oracy. This allows students the opportunity to see and use the target vocabulary in multiple settings in order for them to eventually "own the word."

Virtually, the practice of having students mixing and mingling to schedule appointments with a buddy is more limited. However, this does not mean that pairing strategies are not possible. On the contrary, even though it requires a bit more time on the part of teacher, the rewards are even more significant. With virtual platforms that have breakout rooms the teacher has the option to automatically have students paired or to do it manually. In the second option, it is the teacher who makes the arrangements for student pairing, but the teacher has to manually enter the names in the assigned breakout room. This could be time consuming and somewhat difficult to do while having to teach but there are options to buy time.

Prior to placing students in their respective breakout rooms, have them work on their journals or review the reading assignment, practice vocabulary, or solve math problems, which will be discussed with their partners. Meanwhile, the names of the students can be entered in manually before sending them off to their respective rooms. This process will have to be repeated if the teacher wants to change the pairing arrangements of students. One other option would be to do a combination of manually and automatically placing students in breakout rooms. Either way, students are still interacting and practicing language and SEL skills.

Another option to grouping students that is not well known is to create a comma-separated values (CSV) file. A CSV file is a text file that has a specific format that allows data to be saved in a table-structured format. These can be created by listing names of partners and corresponding room numbers on a Microsoft Excel file but saved in a CSV format that can be uploaded into even before the students sign on. This then becomes the default list for student groupings.

Teachers should always visit the breakout groups and virtual rooms to monitor progress and assist when students are having difficulty connecting, communicating, and sharing equal time. This is another form of formative assessments. For larger virtual groups, teachers have to option to recruit volunteers, whether they be colleagues, parents, or older students, to assist with creating breakout rooms, visiting in the breakout rooms, or even assisting with the delivery of the lesson on Share Screen or links to other instructional platforms.

Cooperative Learning Activities

All prior work in developing and practicing SEL skills, reinforcing Shared Agreements and Norms of (Virtual) Collaboration, participating in morning meetings and community circles, and utilizing pairing strategies, are all precursors to preparing ELs and LTELs to be able to participate effectively and equally in larger cooperative groups of three or four students. ELs at all levels of language proficiency benefit from cooperative learning activities because they can work in small group settings, have multiple opportunities to use language, make mistakes and take risks, and learn from peers who are at various academic and language ability levels.

Cooperative learning activities, when done properly, can achieve 100 percent student participation. This almost guarantees that all students will get to practice SEL competencies and academic content integration, exchange ideas, participate in discourse, and engage in academic dialog to express, summarize, and synthesize information while being included in team and individual accountability. For LTELs, cooperative learning consists of learning strategies that give LTELs easy routines and protocols to engage in productive ways, to practice their social and emotional competencies, academic language, reading fluency and comprehension, and drafting, editing, revising, and publishing. This would provide a great academic boost for LTELs by creating greater opportunities for academic integration with language and literacy and other core content areas. In addition, what better way to explicitly teach, model, and reinforce empathy with English speakers who will be working cooperatively with ELs than through cooperative learning strategies.

Incorporating cooperative learning strategies that emphasize SEL competencies in the content areas allows teachers to check students' understanding of the specific competency to be practiced, what skills need to be retaught, and monitor the degree of their social interaction with other students, especially with LTELs. Placing an added emphasis on enhancing English language acquisition in a safe and supportive learning community will ultimately motivate LTELs to want to participate, interact, and learn at a higher level. This will promote LTELs becoming more academically productive, better behaved, and less likely to drop out. This is a sure way to help ELs and LTELs build social confidence.

Cooperative learning strategies that are effectively used school wide can have the effect of shaping an academic mindset that enhances learning for all students.

1. *Learning norms, protocols, and SEL competencies are reinforced with the expectation that students will practice them during each activity. These behaviors should also include being polite, being respectful, taking turns speaking, helping one another, and accepting help.*
2. *Students are given tasks, not roles, for their performance during each lesson.*
3. *Strategies for cooperative learning, classroom management, and reinforcement of SEL competencies go hand in hand.*

Figure 3.8 Effective Cooperative Learning Strategies

Cooperative learning teams can be created virtually without much difficulty. As with virtual pairing strategies, cooperative teams that are heterogeneous can be created in advance to ensure an equitable distribution of language ability and academic levels. These teams can be created in advance on a CSV file or manually placed into breakout rooms. There are a number of programs and apps out on the market that have the features and capacity to facilitate cooperative learning teams, such as Google Meet, Zoom, Microsoft Teams, and Cisco Webex.

- *Define the learning objectives for the activity.*
- *Assign three or four students to heterogeneous groups with particular attention to balancing out the team with students with various English-language abilities.*
- *Consider assigning students specific roles related to the task to be completed, social skills to be practiced, and a timekeeper.*
- *Teacher monitors the work and evaluates group and individual performance.*
- *Allocate time for students to reflect on their interactions and levels of participation, identify potential improvements for future group work, and complete the assigned task.*

Figure 3.9 Additional cooperative learning strategies

In addition, there are a number of educational apps that can interface with these programs that can further facilitate the sharing of digital content and improve the level of engagement of the students, thus enriching the virtual cooperative learning experience. Some of the programs include Google Docs, Sococo for Classrooms, Teachable, BLEND, Padlet, TodaysMeet, Twilda, Collaborize Classroom, Scribblar, Schoology, Flipgrid, Screencastify, EdPuzzle, and Canvas Teacher.

Teacher Learning Communities

Hybrid or blended teaching/learning has been quite a challenge for all educators. This uncharted territory is going to require a lot of TLC (Tender Loving Care and Teachers' Learning Communities) this school year. Teachers' Learning Communities (TLCs) are spaces where teachers meet for 30 or so minutes, virtually or face-to-face (Calderón 1999).

1. *Check In on one another's well-being and need for emotional support.*
2. *Communicate and collaborate.*
3. *Set a purpose for you, your students, and their families.*
4. *Create a plan—objectives, lesson components, tutorials, with colleagues.*
5. *Model and share successful strategies with colleagues.*
6. *Create and be creative with your favorite colleagues (goes beyond school PLCs).*
7. *Celebrate your growth with your TLC and celebrate on your own.*

Figure 3.10 Steps for effective TLCs

Optimistic Closures consist of reflections on the day, the lesson taught, personal learning, and accomplishments. This gives the learner the opportunity to make meaning of the experience and interactions with others, to look forward to the next gathering, and anticipate what might be learned.

Figure 3.11 Definition of optimistic closures

Optimistic closures could consist of short activities that can be used to check for understanding; emphasize key information at the end of a lesson; and, for ELs and LTELs, reflect on positive experiences with peers and teacher, and express the desire to further build on the positive experience.

Optimistic closures also offer time for reflections on even the most difficult moments, areas that will be addressed or improved on for the next class and reasons for looking forward to having another opportunity to try again.

Students can find optimistic closures helpful by summarizing, reviewing, and demonstrating their understanding of major points; consolidating and internalizing key information; connecting lesson ideas to a previously learned concept or practice; and transferring ideas to new situations. For teachers, optimistic closures allow them to check for understanding and adjust instruction for the next lesson, take a closer look on the progress of LTELs, select SEL competencies and behaviors that need greater emphasis, and address any confusion, incomplete work, or misunderstandings.

The closing activities could be three to five minutes depending on the time available and the need to go deeper into the review process. This is an excellent time for a deeper reflection on the Five Core SEL Competencies. By selecting certain closing activities, students can be more reflective on specific competencies that the activity emphasized. For example, one activity could help them reflect on self-awareness by having them identify emotions and recognize strengths. Another could emphasize self-management by having a student assess their organization skills and goal-setting abilities. For all students this is a great way to reflect in social awareness and how they showed empathy and respect and appreciated the diversity of ELs and LTELs. They could also reflect on their relationship skills and their ability to take the initiative to communicate with other students that they are not familiar with. And, ultimately, they could measure the degree to which they were able to make responsible decisions relative to how they participated, completed tasks, and assisted others in completing their work as well.

One activity that has become popular with both engaging instructional activities and optimistic closure is Give 1, Get 1! This activity is designed to encourage 100 percent participation and promote writing skills, communications, and valuing diverse perspectives on the same experience.

1. *Using the handout, take three to four minutes for students to write three or four significant learnings, strategies, or ideas that they have learned during the class period. They enter one idea per box.*

2. *At the signal students get up and find a partner and begin the process to Get 1 and Give 1 by sharing one idea and receiving one idea or key learning. Each partner should read what they wrote and provide a short explanation. Partners then write down what the other shared on their sheet.*

3. *As with other engaging activities, students should practice formal greetings and expressions of appreciation for sharing. With ELs in particular, students need to continue showing respect, support, and empathy by helping them with the process, even if it means taking the time to copy word by word from each other's paper.*

4. *Continue the mixing and mingling until most students have their sheets filled. Call time with a familiar signal and have students return to their seats.*

5. *Have students share out one idea that really resonated with them and then have them call on the next student to share out. Make sure that ELs and LTELs have an equal chance to share out as well.*

Figure 3.12 Steps for Give One, Get One!

Name:_____   Date:_____

Give 1, Get 1! - Review

Instructions: On your own, write down **four** significant learnings, strategies or ideas you have learned in this session.

Partner sharing: Once you have listed **four**, wonder around the room and share some your ideas with a partner. Add one unique

Figure 3.13 Give 1, Get 1!

The *SEL 3 Signature Practices Playbook* (2019) also contains a number of activities that can be used in the classroom and with some modification could also be done virtually. Some of these include: Future Me, Human Bar Graph, I Am Curious, My Next Step, One-Minute Accolade, One Takeaway I'm Going to Try, One-Word Whip Around, SEL Standards Connections Suit Yourself, and the UFO/Energy Ball (pp. 37–46).

Chapter 4 goes into greater detail on expediting SEL in language through Blended Instruction for LTELs. The strategies in that chapter build skill, confidence, content knowledge, and social and emotional skills. Chapter 5 describes instruction that produces quality reading for different genres and Chapter 6 focuses on writing to expedite learning for LTELs.

Supporting Parents or Caretakers

It is of great importance during these difficult times that schools reach out to parents to support their involvement in the education of their children. We have always known that parental involvement in their child's education greatly benefits students, but it is much more important now than ever. If we want students to continue learning at home and not let the COVID Slide take its toll on increasing the education gap, then we need families to be our partners. That means that our communication with adults who may have limited English proficiency has to be well thought out and followed through.

Since parents want to be kept up to date on the school events and schedules and need assistance with their children's schoolwork, one area to consider is the production of informational and instructional videos and audio recordings with easy explanations on topics of interest to the parents. Volunteers with different language abilities could be sought out to help with the production of these videos and interpreters could be recruited to assist with phone calls as well. Here are some topics to consider for families/guardians.

1. Reassure parents that you care about their child and are there to support them.
2. Ask parents and their children to express their preferences for technology use and communications.
3. Record a tutorial on how to use the new technology, programs, and communications channels.
4. Invite them to visit their children's lessons or practice vocabulary with their children when possible.
5. Produce a recording about the options of student projects that they can do at home that are culturally relevant. These are projects such as documenting in writing or video recording the family history, places where they have lived, an interesting relative, current construction, or repairs at home where they can describe math calculations and logistics. Even going shopping and cooking can turn into creative projects for adolescents.
6. Introduce vocabulary on the topics they choose and send that vocabulary home and ask for parental support to review and practice the vocabulary with their children.
7. How to take time out to do an emotional and personal check-in with their child to see how they are doing and what they could do to take better care of themselves physically and emotionally.

We will describe additional culturally creative projects in the next chapters.

Conclusion

In this chapter we took a deeper look at the SEL Three Signature Practices and incorporated the framework of Welcoming Routines and Rituals, Engaging Pedagogy and Strategies and Optimistic Closures as the guiding outline for the content. This is the perfect tool to organize the broad range of thinking, activities, processes, and strategies needed to effectively integrate SEL practices in creating a failsafe learning environment for ELs and LTELs. Each of the three frameworks included specific practices that were designed to bring LTELs "into the fold." The simple task of establishing shared agreements and norms of (virtual) collaboration are essential in establishing a foundation, an infrastructure, and a template that most students and adults need to help them to become more actively engaged in both face-to-face and virtual learning environments.

Here are some additional practices, suggestions, and resources for teachers:

1. Incorporate SEL activities, resources, and interventions from day one. Students will need to feel accepted, emotionally supported, validated, and cared for by adults and peers whether it be online or in person.

2. Teach LTEL how to communicate with you and their peers through digital platforms, formal emails, and texts (for example, using capital letters and punctuation) and how to talk to teachers via a telephone. Students love to hold pictures of their teacher while they speak on the phone—one to one—with their teacher. Just a few calls a day to different families can do wonders for the students and, most especially, their teachers. Everyone craves human connection beyond a group video call. This should be the responsibility of not only teachers, but every staff member, para-professional, and administrator should be helping teachers make personal connections.

3. Sidewalk visits with safe distancing requires some support, and perhaps some gas money, but while the weather is still good, it is great for teachers to be outside and great for students and families to see and talk with their teachers, if only at a distance.

4. Provide as much consistency, routines, and support on the use of tech tools, virtual lesson designs, and emotional support as possible. Model how to use the technology for both the purpose of academics and developing SEL competencies, such as self-management, social skills, and relationship skills, even if they had already been exposed to virtual learning.

5. Intensive checks for disengaged students are needed. Many students have simply checked out during the months while in quarantine and some will remain checked out even when they return to school. Perhaps they are bored, or they are caring for siblings while parents are at work or they are sharing technology with other siblings or they are taking on manual labor or other jobs to help pay the rent. If we do not first learn why students are disengaged we cannot come up with more innovative solutions to increase their engagement.

6. Collaboration on units, common formative assessments, and parent communication are essential, and there is nothing better than face-to-face, mask-to-mask, communication.

7. Consider using various platforms and apps to create an online bulletin board or discussion board that can be used to display information for any topic, lessons, and videos. Students should also be able to add comments and content.

Personal Reflections and Collegial Discussions

1. Which SEL routines and rituals would you implement immediately, both face-to-face and virtually?

   _____

   _____

2. How would you have students participate in establishing shared agreements and norms?

   _____

   _____

3. How would you use the pairing strategies of Clock Buddies and Academic Vocabulary Buddies?

   _____

   _____

4. Which SEL competencies would need to be explicitly taught to students for them to increase their participation virtually?

   _____

   _____

5. Beyond vocabulary, how would SEL also be integrated into reading and writing?

   _____

   _____

6. What are the programs and apps that you are using in your school for distance learning?

   _____

   _____

7. What challenges are you and your colleagues facing with distance learning in teaching your students and communicating with your parents?

   _____

   _____

Chapter 4

Language in Blended Instruction

if remote teaching perplexes teachers, imagine what remote learning is like for Sandra and other LTELs. Maybe it is not as perplexing for some LTELs, since they have grown up in this country and probably have had some form of technology at home. Yet, we know that is not the case for many, particularly students living in poverty, lacking high-speed Internet, sharing devices, sharing beds, being the current breadwinners. Many LTELs work essential jobs, probably without adequate protection, are taking care of siblings, and are worrying about immigration issues—all reasons they might not have signed on to remote lessons the first time around.

In addition to the myriad of responsibilities and the added stress related to their level of uncertainty for their future and scarcity of resources, LTELs are receiving very little if any financial and emotional support. There are a number of community agencies that are trying to assist but the emotional trauma that many are experiencing will have long-term consequences. Coupled with the extended absence of direct social contact with peers, teachers, and counselors, and six- to eight-month laps in formal education, the perfect storm will more than likely be created for potential large-scale failures and premature dropouts of LTELs. Teachers and administrators are struggling to figure out the best formula for a safe return to school, but the unpredictability of COVID-19 is making definite plans with adequate budgets almost impossible. LTELs need emotional support and a compassionate and empathetic response to their emotional turmoil as well as their material and learning needs.

What Can We Do?

Taking into consideration that uncertainty will continue, here are some suggestions we have collected from schools that are simultaneously focusing on equity and quality instruction for all students. These recommendations parallels those from teachers and educational organizations such as Education Week and the Association for Supervision and Curriculum Development (ASCD), and their EL experts.

1. Prepare for a range of LTEL home experiences, technology barriers, but also the strengths/talents LTEL are developing.

2. Be creative once you find out about your students. Begin planning the SEL activities, resources, and interventions they will need to feel accepted (maybe for the first time), emotionally supported, and cared about by adults and peers online.

3. Design lessons specifically for LTELs. They are at the cusp of becoming excellent students. Do not water down their curriculum by placing them with newcomers or using generic EL programs. Think of Sandra in chapter 1.

4. Begin with lessons that are short, engaging, reflective of their own feelings and experiences, and include topics that LTELs can explore and relate to their own daily lives.

5. Provide as much consistency and maximum support as possible on the use of tools, lesson designs, and emotional support. Plan to model how to use the technology for both the purpose of academics and developing SEL competencies such as relationship skills, even if they had already been exposed to virtual learning.

6. Teach LTELs how to communicate with you and their peers through digital platforms, formal emails, and texts (using capital letters and punctuation) and how to talk to teachers via a telephone. Create some videos with role plays.

7. Even if a new literacy program or format is introduced, students should still have some access to programs they have used before, for comfort in learning until they figure out the new one.

8. If you introduce new specific literacy programs, LTELs should be able to use them at home. Ensure they have access to vocabulary they will need to be successful with the required assignments.

9. If your district is implementing a new self-paced program, help students by creating tutorial videos on how to use the program. Ask them to partner virtually with a peer to share understanding and insights into the new material and to support and motivate one another to complete the work. Your school district should provide the material in the home language as well.

10. Connect and keep constant communication with the LTEL's family. Have the school develop videos in the family's language; add your own flair and personality to go with the generic videos.

11. Ask students to download an assistive technology program that can provide text-reading assistance such as Read&Write. If needed, during synchronous learning, share a screen with a student and walk the student through the process. During the lesson, pre-teach vocabulary and provide questioning and comprehension discourse frames. Students can respond verbally or write in the chat box. They can also send in drawings or pictures to complement their messages.

Figure 4.1 Focusing on Equity for LTEL

Which of these topics are you already covering?

_____

_____

_____

Which do you plan to add?

_____

_____

_____

Figure 4.2 Jot down your reflections to share later with your colleagues

Modeling for Student Comprehension and Language Practice

Your videos can walk students through the process of logging on, answering questions, and submitting answers. For tools such as highlighting or note-taking, create tutorials modeling the use of the tools. Two free programs to use for creating brief videos are Screencastify (https://www.screencastify.com/) and EdPuzzle (https://edpuzzle.com/). Ask students to download an assistive technology program that can provide text-reading assistance, such as Read&Write. If needed, during synchronous learning, share a screen with a student and walk the student through the process. Most teachers like to use cooperative learning teams and send students into breakout rooms during live online lessons to practice in pairs, triads, or teams of four (Calderón and Tartaglia 2020). During the lesson, pre-teach vocabulary and provide questioning and comprehension discourse frames (see examples below). Students can respond verbally or write in the Chat box. They can also send in drawings, pictures, slides, or videos to complement their messages.

Show students how to make their videos. Student videos will be more engaging with a few tips and explanations, such as the following:

- Keep it brief.
- Keep it simple.
- Smile and be nice.
- Look into the camera.
- Practice before you record.
- Avoid words like "ummm," and "OK."
- Be creative; make it fun.

What other language practice activities/strategies do you use?

_____

_____

_____

What else do you plan to add?

_____

_____

_____

Figure 4.3 Jot down your reflections to share later with your colleagues

Scaffolding Remote Learning for LTEL

If your district is using HyperDocs (digital lessons that are created by teachers, for teachers, and fully customizable to meet the needs of learners and teachers) to instruct students, consider that when creating a hyperdoc for English learners, less is more. Too many features or links can be overwhelming and frustrating, and many parts may become missed. A number of EL teachers are not seeing their students engage with the hyperdocs they have created because of overload. Hyperdoc lessons should be accessible and provide scaffolds such as visuals, text-reading assistance, and ease of use for submitting assignments (Calderón and Tartaglia 2020). Another tool is a collaborative online bulletin board. Available from many companies including Padlet, Popplet, and Wakelet, teachers can use an online bulletin board to display information for any topic, lessons, and videos, and students are also able to add comments and content.

What else have you discovered that scaffolds online learning?

_____

_____

_____

What else do you plan to add?

_____

_____

_____

Figure 4.4 Jot down your reflections to share later with your colleagues

Recuperating or Magnifying Language Proficiency

For the past fifteen years, we have conducted research while embedded in schools testing different approaches, models, strategies, and techniques for teaching academic language, reading comprehension and academic writing to develop a framework we call Expediting Comprehension for English Language Learners (ExC-ELL™) (Calderón 2007; Calderón, et al. 2020). Comparison cohorts of matched EL background and proficiency levels were used in the research model. After five years of testing, we found that integrating language, literacy, and content was the most effective way to help all ELs succeed academically, LTELs in particular. This chapter begins with the component that undergirds all the other components: vocabulary. The number of words a student knows and uses in oral and written discourse determines a student's level of reading comprehension, academic knowledge, and success in school and life. According to Graves, August, and Carlo (2011) ELs need to learn from 3,000 to 5,000 words a year so that they can graduate successfully from high school with a total of 50,000 words by the time they graduate from high school.

Teaching Vocabulary as a Precursor to Reading and Learning

Shockingly, we have heard teachers say, "But, my ELs don't read; they can't read," and "They take notes and I read," and "We don't read in math (science, social studies)," and "We watch videos and discuss."

Such comments lead one to conclude that LTELs are not reading enough or not reading at all. A new way of thinking for this new school year would be to start with the idea that LTELs need to learn how to make sense from texts in all subject areas and learn more academic vocabulary. As readers, they have to learn to negotiate all types of text features and text structures. Hence, the role of the teacher is to teach key vocabulary from a text before students start to read as well as additional words during reading and after reading in preparation for good writing. Vocabulary gives LTELs the ability to make sense of what is written in the text, even to understand the definitions included in the context of a text.

Chapter 5 goes into greater detail on expediting reading for LTELs. The strategies in that chapter build skill, confidence, and content knowledge. Chapter 6 describes instruction that produces quality writing for a different genre. In this chapter we concentrate on vocabulary as the basis for reading and writing.

Selecting Words from a Text—Any Text

The words to teach come from the text students are about to read during that day's lesson. Beck, McKeown, and Kucan (2002) introduced the concept of three different types of words that exist in all the texts: Tier 1, Tier 2, and Tier 3. The Tier 1 words are those easy everyday words a native English speaker knows by second grade, but a few LTELs might have superficial knowledge or not know some of those words. Tier 2 words are the ones that will give the teacher and student the most mileage. These are the most frequent words in texts and tests. In *Teaching and Learning Vocabulary: Bringing Research to Practice* (2005), Beck and colleagues provided more detail to the three tiers. In that same compendium, Calderón and colleagues expanded the three-tiers framework to address the specific needs of ELs (Calderón, et al. 2005). For ELs, Tier 2 words are those that nest the Tier 3 words and create contextual difficulty of meaning for ELs. Tier 3 words are subject-specific words that teach the concepts for a particular discipline and are what students are tested on. However, without knowing the Tier 2 words that are in the test questions, LTELs may not answer correctly even if they know the concept. Test questions have many Tier 2 words and phrases that can support LTEL comprehension. Therefore, we emphasize the importance of focusing instruction on these words in a certain routine described after the tiers.

Tiers 2 and 3 also include SEL words to be used during explicit SEL instruction, whether they be in a specific lesson from an evidence-based SEL program or words that define specific actions and discourse that will be highlighted and practiced during pairing or cooperative learning activities.

TIER 3: Subject-specific words that label content discipline concepts, subjects, emotions, and topics. These are key words, albeit infrequently used academic ones (for example, "carbon dioxide," "photosynthesis," "constitutional rights," "computability," and "foreshadowing").

For current topics or learning and applying SEL competencies, you might want to add to the typical Tier 3 words that texts highlight in bold or that are to be found in the glossary:

1. COVID-19—coronavirus, global pandemic, quarantine, sequestered, stay-at-home orders, reopening, CDC Guidelines, job and food insecurity, vaccine, antibodies, first responders, essential personnel, unemployment, trauma, bankruptcy, stock market, facemasks, distancing, PPE—Personal Protective Equipment.
2. Virtual learning—hybrid, blended learning, synchronous, asynchronous, online classes, Zoom, Google Meets, Microsoft Teams and Cisco Webex connectivity, promotions and graduation, grading, hardware.
3. Racial and Political arena—social unrest, constitutional right to peaceful protest, racism, white privilege, use of excessive force, and Black Lives Matter.
4. Social and emotional learning (SEL)Self-Awareness, Self-Management, Social Skills, Relationship Skills, Responsible Decision Making, empathy, compassion, kindness, respect, resiliency, grit, persistence, separation anxiety, stress, anger, depression, conflict resolution, restorative practices, valuing diversity, perspective taking, goal setting, communication skills, and consequences of actions.

TIER 2: Information processing words that nest Tier 3 words in long sentences; polysemous words; transition words; connectors; more sophisticated words for rich discussions and specificity in descriptions; phrases; sentence starters; cognates; false cognates; idioms; and other linguistic structures that create problems for ELs. (More examples are provided below.)

TIER 1: Basic words that ELs need to communicate, read, and write. Those that might be necessary for LTELs because they might have missed the specific meaning (for example, "leg" in leg of a lap, branch of a math sequence, or leg of a table); how the word is used across several idioms (no leg to stand on, on one's last legs, shake a leg); they are still having problems with pronunciation (for example, "tooth," "toothache," "phrase"); or they are struggling with differentiating homonyms (for example, "there," "their," "they're").

Tier 3 Words

The following are slides from our face-to-face and virtual presentations that are more frequently requested by our participants. We hope you share this information with your LTEL because they will benefit from having them on hand in virtual folders or on table tents if/when possible. Feel free to share with your colleagues and have discussions about how to use these or what other similar patterns can be given to the students. You can also download other tools at www.exc-ell.com.

Tier 3 words, especially in more complex and higher-level texts, are typically defined within long sentences, or in the glossary, or explained with illustrations, graphs, charts, and other text features. They are also highlighted with bold letters in the text and, of course, found in accountability tests. Sometimes they are called academic words. Albeit when they are nested in complex Tier 2 words, hence those Tier 2 words can also be called academic. They uphold the Tier 3 words.

MATH	SCIENCE	SOCIAL STUDIES
Square root	Photosynthesis	Government
Rectangle	Germ	Bylaws
Radical numbers	Atom	Ballot
Circumference	Matter	Congressional
Pi	Osmosis	Capital
Power	Power	Power

Table 4.1 TIER 3 Subject Specific Words

Tier 3
words

1. _____
2. _____
3. _____
4. _____
5. _____
6. _____

Figure 4.5 What are six Tier 3 words from your subject area?

Tier 3 words are subject-specific words that represent the topic of study. Depending on the grade level, "money" can be the Tier 3 word in second grade because it is the topic of the article. In fifth grade, "wealth" might be used as the Tier 3 topic, and "capital" could be the topic of an article in a seventh grade text. Words for a similar concept fit for different grade levels. For LTEL, we could request fidelity to the text semantics because when they are discussing or writing, and they have already encountered the higher-level word, it could be a reminder to use the one from the text (instead of *jar*, use *beaker)*.

Academic Content Words by Levels of Difficulty		
Jar	Container	Beaker
Shape	Rectangle	Quadrilateral
Money	Wealth	Capital
Person	Character	Protagonist
People	Population	Demographics

Table 4.3 SEL Tier 3 Words

SEL Content Specific Words from a Yale Mood Meter

Red	Blue	Green	Yellow
Enraged	Bored	Calm	Happy
Angry	Disappointed	Pleasant	Motivated
Annoyed	Depressed	Gratified	Elated
Stressed	Alienated	Blessed	Astonished
Concerned	Discouraged	Contemplative	Hyper
Anxious	Drained	Tranquil	Pleased
Stunned	Sad	Peaceful	Blissful

Table 4.2 Levels of Text Difficulty

Tier 3 words

1.
2.
3.
4.
5.
6.
7.
8.
9.
10.

Figure 4.6 What are some Tier 3 words in your texts?

Tier 2 Words

Tier 2 words are those that are rarely pointed out in core-content texts but create more comprehension problems than the Tier 3 words. These are the words and phrases that nest the Tier 3 words. If students do not know those words, the meaning of a Tier 3 word will be lost. In addition to nesting and defining Tier 3 words, Tier 2 words are prevalent in discussions, videos, websites, and academic writing.

For instance, in the following passage we highlight the Tier 2 words. Students will encounter many Tier 2 words and clusters throughout the whole text that are necessary to learn about what is causing climate change. The underlined words illustrate the abundancy of Tier 2 in a science text:

Natural causes <u>alone</u>, <u>however</u>, cannot explain all of these changes. Human activities <u>which have been noted as contributing to</u> climate change, are <u>primarily due</u> to the <u>release</u> of billions of tons of carbon dioxide (CO_2) and other heat-trapping gases, <u>known as</u> greenhouse gases, into the atmosphere every year.

Tier 2 Words in State Exams

Common Tier 2 words found in State exams, as well as core content textbooks, are often overlooked in glossaries or highlighted texts:

absence, accuracy, additive, affect, allow, analogous, apparent, approach, arrange, assortment, assumption, bases, basis, behavior, belief, body, boundary, coincide, compiled, core, criteria, crucial, denote, depict, deplete, device, display, distinct, due to, effect, forthcoming, generate, illustrate, impact, implicit, notwithstanding, oddly, so that, solely, state, successive, underlying, vary, whereby, widespread . . .

Most of the time, these are found as a single word. Nevertheless, they might be found as phrases or clusters (for example, barely apparent, primarily due to, oddly enough).

Polysemous Words

Other troublemakers are the polysemous words—words that have multiple meanings across the subject areas.

- An LTEL might have heard "table" in the ESL classroom as a place where you eat your meals.
- When she goes to science, I wonder what picture she forms in her head for a water table?
- Her algebra teacher says use a table to write out that equation.
- Her government teacher says, just as Lorena is finally brave enough to raise her hand, "Let's table this discussion. It's time for lunch."

POLYSEMOUS WORDS Across Academic Content Areas			
Solution	Power	Fall	Down
Table	Cell	Check	Drained
Divide	Right	Court	Spent
Prime	Radical	Long	Hyper
Round	Leg	Pin	Composed
Trunk	Left	Rest	Trying
State	Light	Roll	Shares
Bank	Face	Hand	Match

Table 4.3 SEL Tier 2 Words

Tier 2 words are the most powerful words. These are words that students can use for life. Unless a student is a biology major, there is little chance that "osmosis" or "photosynthesis" will pop up in their discourse. Nevertheless, the transition and connecting words in the graph below will probably be used over and over.

Tier 2 Transition and Connecting Words

There is another benefit for concentrating on teaching Tier 2 words before, during and after reading. Transition words and those that connect two or more thoughts enhance class discussions and writing. When the concept of transition and connectors is introduced, it is fine for students to use words such as "because," "and," "or," "but," or "for example." However, after two weeks, inform the students that they can no longer use those words; instead, they must use words such as "as a result," "in contrast," "in addition," and "for instance." After a few more weeks, inform them that they can no longer use those words. In their place, introduce "so that," "nevertheless," "moreover," and "in particular." Thus, you can continue to add more every two weeks or so.

The key concept here is that LTEL realize, perhaps for the first time, that they are being held accountable for learning and using new, more sophisticated, words, systematically. Check their writing at the end of each learning period to make sure they are applying those words correctly and frequently. Keep a log of their use during discussions or peer summarizations. Authentic (on the spot) or performance assessment will tell you much more than the typical paper and pencil vocabulary tests.

Tier 2 Learning Progressions with Connectors
Cause and Effect—because, due to, as a result, since, for this reson, therefore, in order to, so that, thus
Contrast—or, but, although, however, in contrast, nevertheless, on the other hand, while...
Addition or Comparison—and, also, as well as, in addition, likewise, moreover, by the way
Giving examples—for example, for instance, in particular, such as, to illustrate

Table 4.5 Tracking Language Learning Progressions with Tier 2

How do you keep track of learning progressions through vocabulary?

_____

_____

_____

How would you implement the Tier 2 Learning Progressions?

_____

_____

_____

Figure 4.7 Jot down your reflections to share later with your colleagues

Phrases, Question Stems, and Sentence Starters are Tier 2

We take the liberty of including these in the Tier 2 categories in order to bring them to prominence. We tend to think that students do not ask questions because they are shy. When I interview students, they tell me that they don't know how to ask questions. These question starters will help them get started. They can keep them in online or hard copy folders.

Can you help me _____?

I don't understand _____.

Where is/are _____?

How do I _____?

May I ask a question?

How much time do we have for _____?

Where do I _____?

Would you please repeat that?

Figure 4.8 Sample basic question starters

In addition to using transition words during discussions, LTEL can express themselves more eloquently with help from sentence starters.

Discussion Sentence Starters

Summarizing: Students create a new oral text that stands for an existing text. The summary contains the important information or big ideas.

This story tells about a . . .

This section is about the . . .

One important fact here is that . . .

The main ideas and attributes are . . .

Determining important information: Students tell the most important idea in a section of text, distinguishing it from details that tell more about it.

The main idea is . . .

The key details that support that are . . .

The purpose of this text is to . . .

Some SEL Interaction Starters:

The reason I feel that way is that . . .

I'm thinking that it is going to be too difficult because . . .

Can we discuss this?

My apologies, I didn't mean . . .

How can we solve this?

What are six Tier 2 words or phrases commonly used in your subject area? Which would you like to see in your students' writing?

Tier 2
words
1. _____
2. _____
3. _____
4. _____
5. _____
6. _____
7. _____
8. _____
9. _____
10. _____

Figure 4.9 Tier 2 words

Tier 1 Words

These words might seem too easy for LTELs who have been in schools more than six years. Nonetheless, sound-spelling correlation for words such as "tough" and "highlight" might have been omitted from their instruction. If they were taught in phonics lessons, as sight word practice, devoid of meaning or context, it is not surprising that they do not recognize them in writing or in speech.

Tier 1 for Newcomers and Some LTELs	
Spelling	tough, toothache, phrase, highlight, because
Pronunciation or confusion with homophones	weather/whether, sum/some, whole/hole, blue/blew, access/exes/axis, sell/cell, ship/chip
Background knowledge	lawnmower, blender, parka, skyscraper
Fale cognates	exit, character, embarrassed, success

Table 4.6 Tier 1 words that create problems for newcomers and some LTELs

In Tier 1 categories, pronunciation of or awareness of homophones, lack of background experiences, or knowledge of items such as a parka or false cognates (words that sound like words in English but do not mean the same thing) might have to be clarified. For instance: character is *personaje* in Spanish when it comes to literature but *carácter* does mean a person's character in a different context: *tiene un carácter muy fuerte* (has a strong personality).

The recommendations for selecting words to preteach and teach later on during the lesson are the same for face-to-face, virtual, or blended lessons. At first, it might seem a time-consuming or complicated task to choose words from all the texts, videos, lab instructions, and so forth that LTELs will read. The good news is that very soon the advantages become evident. This success and continuous practice with the teacher and peers will also propel students to use the same sequence we see below for learning words on their own.

Preteaching Tier 2 Vocabulary: Face-to-Face

Five or six words/phrases/clusters should be selected to preteach before students read, watch a video, and/or listen to new information. Each word/phrase/cluster can be taught in two minutes: one minute for teacher to present the first five steps to help students understand the word in the context where it will be found, and one minute for students to practice in pairs using the new word/phrase with a partner.

Before teaching each word with the 7 Steps below teachers begin by discussing and modeling how to practice the social norms and shared agreements with their learning buddy.

---

1. Teacher says the word (or phrase) and asks students to repeat the word three times after the teacher.
2. Teacher states the word in context from text.
3. Teacher provides the dictionary definition.
4. Teacher provides student-friendly definition.
5. Teacher highlights grammar, spelling, polysemy, and so on.
6 ➔ *Students engage in teacher-provided sentence starter or frame using the target vocabulary for 60 seconds.*
7. Teacher informs students how/when to use the word in peer summaries, Exit Passes, or other writing assignments.

Figure 4.10 The seven steps for preteaching a word (Calderón 2007b, 2018, 2020)

Teachers find that writing out the steps on Microsoft PowerPoint for the seven steps helps the students understand the sequence and become accustomed to the routine. The teacher's steps 1 to 5 should be written on a PowerPoint or Google slide. This helps the teacher explain the meaning in one minute or maybe two at the most. Step 1 is critical because this is where LTELs learn the correct pronunciation of the words. In Step 2, the whole sentence where the word is found is written in the mentor text. Step 3 provides the correct dictionary definition. The teacher provides it. If it is a polysemous word, the students might select the wrong definition. Sometimes the dictionary definition is quite difficult, but LTELs need to be exposed to academic language. With Step 4, the teacher provides a student-friendly definition to make sure that the student understands the correct meaning. In Step 5, something about the word can be briefly stated: it is in the past tense, it is a polysemous word or a cognate or an idiom; notice the prefix, suffix, or root word.

Step 6 is for pairs of students to practice using the word with their own examples for one whole minute. Each should provide about five or six examples in one minute. A sentence starter or frame is provided by the teacher to make sure that they use the word in a complete sentence, not just a one-word response. This is a good opportunity to practice listening—as they listen to the partners' responses. It gives the teacher useful data to record and compare over time, to gauge how the LTEL is progressing in verbal fluency, sentence construction, and use of academic vocabulary. This is better than the typical vocabulary test where students match definition and word—where it is easy to guess the answers—and not have depth of meaning.

Step 6 Develops SEL

Step 6 is also an excellent opportunity to take into consideration the diverse needs of ELs and pair them in the best possible way. This can be done by pairing them manually during online learning or by using pairing tools such as the AVB. Step 6 is where social norms and shared agreements are practiced reinforcing:

- turn taking

- empathic listening

- building positive relationships

- valuing diversity of option

- asking for help/offer help

Figure 4.11 Norms of interaction with learning partners (Calderón 2017, 2018, 2020)

Rewarding the student's effort to practice these behaviors will contribute greatly to an LTEL's self-confidence and willingness to participate in class activities. This adds to their belief that the classroom, whether face-to-face or virtual, is a safe and secure place to participate where they can ask for help and receive support from all students in the class. One great example would be when an EL is unable to think of an original sentence during pair share, the other student assists in creating a sentence or has the EL repeat the partner's sentence. This example speaks volumes of how students have internalized the SEL competencies of empathy, compassion, relationship skills and responsible decision-making.

Finally, Step 7 is called the accountability step. This is where the teacher reminds the students where and when they are to use the word: in their partner oral summaries, in their written summaries, on a writing assignment.

As you prepare your student pairs before you teach the 7 Steps, what are some social norms that you would ask them to adhere to?

Step six norms	1.
	2.
	3.
	4.
	5.
	6.

Figure 4.12 Social norms to adhere to

Select a Tier 2 word or phrase from your text and map out the 7 Steps.

Word:	1.
	2.
	3.
	4.
	5.
	6.
	7.

Figure 4.13 Map out the 7 Steps (Calderón 2007b, 2018, 2020)

If there is a lengthy passage they need to read, consider chunking the text and teaching it in separate close-reading lessons. You can select five or six words from each chunk to preteach before the students begin their reading.

Preteaching Tier 2 Vocabulary Virtually

The process and routine described above is easily adaptable for distance learning. Here are specific ways to model, have your LTEL practice, give them feedback, and hold them accountable for using the word in follow-up activities. Before you preteach vocabulary online, break up the text and select key five or six words/phrases to preteach before ELs read or work on assignments from each text segment. Look for information-processing vocabulary that will facilitate comprehension of key concepts, words like "in retrospect," "controversial," and "over the course of." Point out polysemous/multiple-meaning words that LTELs might take for granted or feel that they already know, such as "left" (meaning direction, exited, left behind, or a political inclination) related idioms ("leftovers," "out in left field," etc.) or SEL-related vocabulary (expressions of emotion, feelings, and thoughts). The vocabulary steps should clarify which meaning is the most appropriate for working with the text.

- Make a video tutorial for students on how to learn a word. Model the steps with your own child or spouse or virtually "gather" a group of ELs using these five steps to learn the word "however"; then, later add the formal dictionary definition and some grammatical feature of the word.

    1. Say the word "however" to yourself or a friend three times.

    2. Here's a friendly definition.
       Another word for "however" is "but."

    3. Here's an example in a sentence.
       I want to go outside; "however," I know we have to stay indoors.

    4. Try five or six examples using the frame to form a sentence.
       I want to _____; however, I _____.

    5. Use this word when you summarize the text with your partner and later in your writing.

- Record their use of the word and the quality of their sentences. Give students feedback, especially if they did a "great" job, but be specific as to what was "great." In addition, acknowledge their effort and in an SEL kind of way show that they are quite capable of expanding their knowledge and language acquisition with practice and support from the teacher and peers. This is a Growth-Mindset approach to building confidence.

- If the students want to record their practice, they can make a video with their laptop, tablet, or smart phone. They can practice with peers during a video chat. Be sure to assign partners.

- Model preparing and using a virtual toolbox to store their new vocabulary, the visuals you provide, and other vocabulary learning tools such as Tier 1, 2, and 3 examples, transition words, false cognates, and other graphics that might be useful during reading and writing. Shared online folders or collaborative online bulletin boards are two ways to create a virtual toolbox.

- Once the students have developed a warehouse full of vocabulary, the learning environment should be emotionally safe enough for LTELs to share and practice their new words. This practice must be planned, done intentionally, and practiced often.

Conclusion: Keep Using the Words

Students need to know that they will need to use those words during their Partner Reading and Verbal Summarization after each paragraph. As they read with their partner, they will recognize the words that were pretaught and those few words will help them figure out the meaning of other new words in the paragraph. As they jointly summarize after each paragraph, they will use those words and new ones they have learned in context. Later in the lesson, they use the words to formulate questions and to do a series of follow-up cooperative activities where they anchor the meaning. When it is time to write academic compositions, they will have mastered those and many more words. Their writing will reflect all the vocabulary they have learned.

The chapters that follow will elaborate on reading and writing sequences and the SEL competencies that they develop concomitantly.

Personal Reflections and Collegial Discussions

1. How many words are the ESL, biology, history, algebra, engineering, language arts, and elective teachers teaching per year?

   _____

   _____

   _____

2. What can we do to teach more vocabulary to LTELs and other striving students?

   _____

   _____

   _____

3. What SEL competencies do we want to build into Step 6?

   _____

   _____

   _____

4. What discourse/discussion tools can we provide for LTELs?

   _____

   _____

   _____

5. How do we incorporate the recommendations listed in Table 4.6, Figure 4.10, and Figure 4.11?

   _____

   _____

   _____

Figure 4.14 Jot down a few thoughts in preparation for conversations with colleagues

Chapter 5

Quality Reading Instruction: The Greatest Gift We Can Give

Reading reform means investing in teachers, giving them effective tools and strategies to ensure that every child gets a firm phonetic base as well as strategies to comprehend all sorts of texts, to build fluency, to develop vocabulary, and most importantly, to love to read.

—*Robert Slavin (2019)*

Some experts estimate that students will lose 30 percent of their annual reading gains and up to 50 percent of their math gains due to the so-called COVID slide. (Migration Policy institute 2020). Is it time for another reform based on science? This is a great opportunity to rebuild our reading programs. The "reading wars" in the last twenty years (phonics versus no phonics, whole language versus scientific view, too many cues and scaffolding) have created huge reading gaps for many students (Calderón and Minaya-Rowe 2011; Moats 2020). Moats also states that the widespread misunderstanding and misapplication of the scientific process of reading continues to create reading failure and declining scores in the National Assessment of Educational Progress (NAEP) and on international comparisons. In chapter two we listed the causes and consequences of the reading wars on LTELs. This is the perfect time to revisit the science of reading and build a consensus to guide instruction from here on.

In addition to taking a serious look at the science of reading, one must be kept in mind that the selection of reading content should complement the teaching of academic language and reading skills, especially during these difficult times. Greater consideration should be given to selecting reading materials that motivate students to want to read because they include relevant and significant learning opportunities for both academic and personal development. The content should also include broader social and emotional competencies, such as interacting with diverse individuals and groups in socially skilled and respectful ways; practicing positive, safe, and healthy behaviors; and contributing responsibly and ethically to their peers, family, school, and community (CASEL 2019a, 2019b).

Reading content that has embedded SEL lessons motivates ELs and LTELs to want to learn to read so they can read to learn. Texts that motivate students to read reflect their stories, histories, and experiences. When schools promote SEL and student voice, and facilitate the interaction with English-dominant peers, there will be greater interest among all students to apply the knowledge, attitudes, and skills to understand and manage emotions, set and achieve positive goals, feel and show empathy for others, establish and maintain positive relationships, and make responsible decisions. In spite of all the setbacks, ELs and LTELs have the ability to develop personal strengths including resiliency, tenacity, perseverance, and positive academic mindsets given the right reading materials, reading strategies, and inclusive instructional practices.

Dr. Slavin's message from 2009 written above is still being disregarded in so many schools and curriculum materials in vogue. Bob has spent his life studying and implementing effective reading programs because he realized from reviews of empirical studies that the quality of reading instruction can mean the difference between success and failure. His compilation of studies is in a Johns Hopkins website (www.bestevidence.org). Findings from that *Best Evidence Encyclopedia* have great implications for LTEL. Here are five fundamental findings and the way we have integrated them into effective reading instructions for LTELs.

(1) Phonics is necessary but not sufficient for effective reading programs. Most of the textbooks and computer-assisted instruction (CAI) software have never been evaluated. Hence simply adopting a different book, curriculum, or CAI made little difference in reading outcomes.
   o In our studies with ELs/LTELs we have found the same problem in phonics programs where ELs parrot nonsense sounds without connecting sound–word meaning. Moreover, most EL texts tend to water down the vocabulary, content knowledge, and metacognitive instruction, facilitating the growing number of LTELs who go on to middle, then, high school.

(2) Cooperative learning methods are important in which students work in pairs or teams of four and tutor one another in phonics skills, help one another learn study skills, and take turns reading to one another and work on meaning.
   o We consistently find that Partner Reading + summarization has the biggest impact on reading for K–12 ELs and LTELs.

(3) Metacognitive strategy instruction is important in which students are taught methods for understanding what they read, such as summarizing, making graphic organizers to represent key ideas, and predicting what will happen next.

  ○ We will share cognitive, metacognitive, and SEL strategies as part of reading for LTELs in this chapter.

(4) Classroom management and motivation training is important along with these strategies that train and coach teachers in methods of organizing classrooms, effectively engaging all students, using time effectively, and having a rapid pace of teaching.

  ○ Due to the unfortunate past history of separating ELs from the general education students, class management and SEL strategies will be absolutely necessary for cooperative learning to work.

(5) For struggling readers, Dr. Slavin found these programs: Peer-Assisted Learning Strategies (PALS), Reciprocal Teaching, Cooperative Integrated Reading and Composition® (CIRC®), READ 180®, and the comprehensive program Success for All (Slavin & Madden 2001).

  ○ A five-year study found the Bilingual Cooperative Integrated Reading and Composition (BCIRC) used in English and Spanish at the elementary level effectively exited ELs by fourth or fifth grade levels and prevented sending LTELs into middle school. The program is listed in the US Department of Education's What Works Clearinghouse (WWC). The results of the study are published in Calderón, Hertz-Lazarowitz and Slavin (1998).

  ○ The professional development program for a comprehensive reading approach is called Expediting Reading Comprehension for English Language Learners (ExC-ELL-TM), which is the basis of this book, was patterned after the BCIRC components but designed for LTELs in middle and high schools, and had school-wide success for the experimental schools in New York City and Kauai, Hawaii (Calderón 2007a). Although originally designed for LTELs in core content classrooms, the schools have found that it works for all students, even those in advanced placement classes.

  ○ A tutoring after-school and/or summer school reading program called Reading Instructional Goals for Older Readers (RIGOR) with student texts in English and Spanish was also compared with other programs in twenty-four middle and high schools in New York City showing greater results than the control programs (Calderón 2007b).

Struggling adolescent readers and LTELs present a particular challenge for core content teachers, as without adequate literacy skills, they cannot succeed in their subject areas. Kennedy and Deshler (2010) found that the more students are exposed to texts, their vocabulary and background knowledge grow, and they become more proficient readers. They found that students at the tenth percentile read about 60,000 words a year. Students at the fiftieth percentile read about 900,000. They recommend the following:

- Give students a wide variety of interesting reading materials at various reading levels.
- Teach students to set their own learning goals.

- Provide ample interaction opportunities with peers to enhance comprehension.
- Identify appropriate comprehension strategies for their content area.
- Model how these strategies should be used to understand subject-specific text.
- Provide multiple opportunities to practice using the strategies.
- Provide feedback to students on their application of the strategies.
- Actively involve students in discussions.
- Instruction in word analysis, reading fluency or vocabulary building.
- Set expectations for using the strategies across all subjects.
- Make improved literacy performance a priority for the entire school staff (Kennedy and Deshler, 2010)).
  - Additionally, for LTELs we recommend that you give them, as often as possible, a voice in choosing texts to read on the topic at hand.
  - Starting a semester with their choice of cultural multimodal texts since it creates more enthusiasm and engagement in reading throughout the semester.
  - Select authentic literature representing cultural and linguistic diversity.
  - Provide websites with multiple language texts.
  - Ensure texts are culturally sensitive, avoiding stereotypes.

Which of these is your school currently implementing?

_____

_____

_____

Which might you and your colleagues want to add to your curriculum?

_____

_____

_____

Figure 5.1 Jot down your reflections to share later with your colleagues

Taking a closer look at integration of CCSS and SEL, according to Hakuta (2011), CCSS requires students to engage deeply in much more complex text than most have been exposed to previously. LTELs should not just read a text, but deeply engage in its vocabulary, point of view, and author's intent, all while connecting to prior knowledge and prior reading.

Students will experience...	And so many need...
longer periods of engagement with text	• self-control as they get wiggly (Self-Management) • self-motivation to stay engaged with the text (Self-Management) • perspective-taking as they make meaning of the text (Social Awareness)
frustration with unfamiliar vocabulary or more complex text structure	• to seek help if they struggle with longer passages unfamiliar vocabulary and structure (Relationship Skills) • to manage stress as they encounter more unfamiliar vocabulary than before (Self-Management) • empathy for classmates who are struggling (Social Awareness)
increased frequency working with peer groups to examine and problem solve around text	• to set and achieve goals (Self-Management) • to understand social and ethical norms for behavior when working in peer groups (Social Awareness) • to communicate clearly and work cooperatively with peers (Relationship Skills) • to considering the well-being of self and others (Responsible Decision-Making)

Table 5.1 Challenges Build Reading Skills and SEL Competencies

Which of the SEL skills are already incorporated into the reading curriculum of all subject areas?

_____

_____

_____

What can you and your colleagues do to increase more SEL development in all subject areas?

_____

_____

_____

Figure 5.2 Jot down your reflections to share later with your colleagues

How to Build the Language, Literacy, Content, and SEL Framework

We took the basic findings from evidence-based research and built ExC-ELLTM. With funding from the US Department of Education's Institute of Education Science and the Carnegie Corporation of New York, we took each strategy and tested it in middle and high school content classrooms. For five years, we compared strategies for teaching vocabulary, reading comprehension, and writing with the popular strategies for teaching ELs in those domains. Once the framework was completed, we tested the whole sequence of twelve components and compared the framework with existing popular EL programs. We used matched control groups in middle and high schools with different student language populations (Spanish, Chinese, Marshallese, and other languages). The LTELs and newcomers in the ExC-ELL™ schools consistently outperformed ELs/LTELs in the control schools. We brought up schools that had been underperforming to schools of excellence. With a National Professional Development grant from the US Department of Education's Office of English Language Acquisition, we continue to study and refine ExC-ELL™ as a whole-school comprehensive program and as a blended program. The twelve components that form the framework are as follows. The following are the 12 Components.

1. Preteaching of Vocabulary
2. Teacher Think-Alouds
3. Student Peer Reading
4. Peer Summaries
5. Depth of Word Studies/Grammar
6. Class Debriefings/Discussions
7. Cooperative Learning Activities
8. Formulating Questions and Numbered Heads
9. Round Table Reviews
10. Pre-writing and Drafting
11. Revising/Editing
12. Reading Final Product

Figure 5.3 The 12 Components of an ExC-ELL™ lesson

The components will be explained throughout the following chapters. Chapter 4 dealt with component one. This chapter focuses on reading components two to nine and more connections between vocabulary and reading. First, the ideal reading program would begin with training on vocabulary instruction as described in the previous chapter. The aim of vocabulary instruction is to increase students' knowledge of the meanings of specific words as they read. Vocabulary knowledge is closely correlated with reading comprehension (Nation 2009), and there are scientific studies in which words have been taught thoroughly enough to raise reading comprehension (NICHD 2000). Knowing the meanings of words matters, but it goes beyond just words. Students need to develop a word conscience (Nagy 2007). Good readers develop word conscience or semantic awareness as we call it in ExC-ELL™. This means trying to figure out a word through morphological analysis (looking for cognates, false cognates, collocations, polysemous words, sophisticated words for specificity, prefixes, suffixes, root words). Nagy (2005) also found that this type of metalinguistic knowledge contributes to reading comprehension. Whether we call it word conscience, semantic awareness, or metalinguistic knowledge what is important is that we provide opportunities for LTELs to develop semantic awareness—self-awareness that their vocabulary must grow on a daily basis. Vocabulary conscience includes the development of reading stamina even in low vocabulary knowledge situations. We can help LTELs by simply encouraging an interest in words and having them read read read in all subjects.

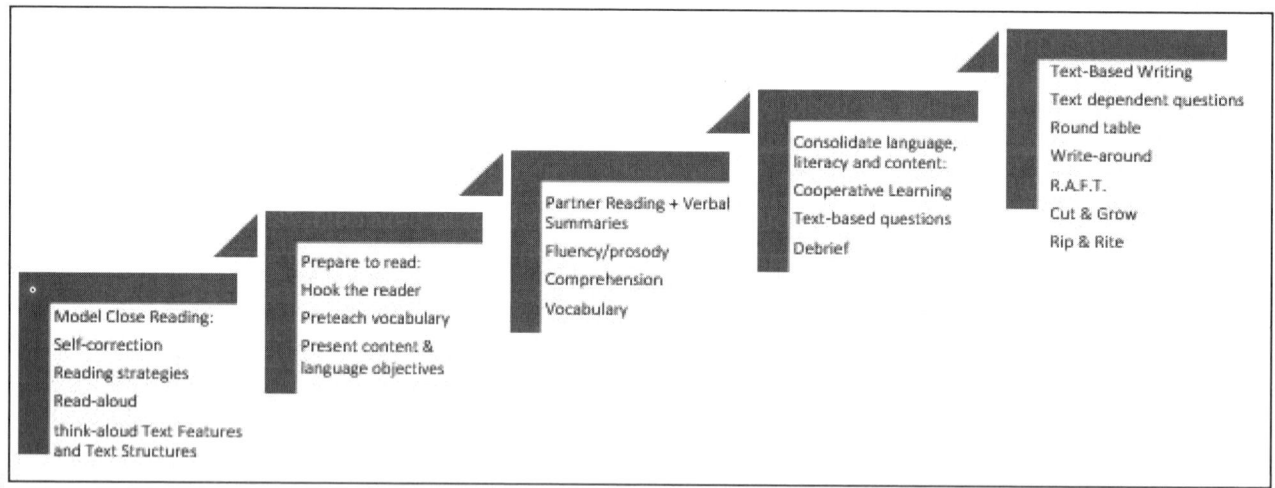

Source: Calderón 2007

Figure 5.4 Five building blocks for reading proficiency

The Five Building Blocks for Reading Proficiency

This chapter will present the instructional strategies for four of the building blocks. The fifth building block, writing, will be mapped out in Chapter 6.

(1) Get Ready—Prepare to Read
- Hook the reader
- Preteach vocabulary
- Present objectives

(2) Model Close Reading
- Self-correction
- Reading strategies
- Read-aloud
- Think-aloud

(3) Practice Close Reading: Partner Reading with Oral Summaries
- Fluency
- Comprehension
- Vocabulary

(4) Anchor Knowledge: Consolidate Language, Literacy, and Content
- Debrief
- Text-based questions
- Cooperative learning activities

(5) Text-Based Writing: Connect Reading and Writing
- Text dependent questions
- Round table
- Write-around
- R.A.F.T.
- Cut & Grow
- Rip & Rite

Source: Calderón 2007

Figure 5.5 Teaching the Five ExC-ELL™ Reading Components

1. Planning for Reading Comprehension

Before teaching the five components, planning on integrating reading into a content area begins by parsing the text that is required or finding a better replacement. Once selected, the text needs to be parsed/analyzed for several purposes.

Reasons for Parsing a Text

(1)   Selecting a content and language standard or objective.

(2)   Identifying the vocabulary that we want the students to learn and use for the rest of the lesson's activities.

(3)   Chunking the text into student manageable parts.

(4)   Identifying the level of sentence complexity and finding a representative sentence whose parts can be signaled out to students and asking students to use a similar sentence structure in their writing later on.

(5)   Identifying comprehension strategies to model through think-alouds.

(6)   Planning how to introduce the text features (illustrations, captions, bullets, italics, quotation marks, hyperlinks, footnotes, glossaries, pop-up dictionaries, citations, headings, subheadings, timelines, sidebars, diagrams, literary devices, punctuation, index and so forth).

(7)   Planning how to introduce the text structures/author's purpose (for example, to inform, convince, argue a point, show cause and effect, discuss a problem and a solution).

(8)   Determining how to pair the students for Partner Reading + Partner Summaries and the sections of the text for Partner Reading and Summarization.

(9)   Selecting language, literacy, and content anchoring activities after reading.

(10)   Formulating questions introduces academic writing

Figure 5.6 What we parse a text for

Take time to review these 10 characteristics with your colleagues. Take a poll—which are more important for your LTEL to do well in your subjects?

_____

_____

_____

Determine on a course of action for including them in your instructional practices.

_____

_____

_____

Figure 5.7 Some reflection questions to share with your colleagues

2. Teacher Models Close Reading through Think-alouds

Teachers can conduct think-alouds to model strategic reading. By thinking aloud about the text features, a teacher can provide background knowledge necessary for the text. For example: This timeline tells me that these historical events took place over a forty-year span. This illustration looks like a medieval castle. Let's see, the medieval era was from about . . . to . . . Here is a painting of a king. I wonder who that king was and why he is part of history.

- Point to one reading comprehension strategy relevant to the text (how to find evidence, cause and effect, and so forth) by highlighting and labeling each instance of using it during your think-aloud.

- Show text features (bullets, graphs, subtitles, etc.) and discuss why they are important for comprehending that text—and for students' later writing.

- The Think Aloud should not take more than three or four minutes.

By reading the first paragraph of a text, a teacher can model the reading comprehension strategy that will be most prevalent throughout the text or meets the objective such as; *determine important information, summarize, determine the cause and the effect, the problem and possible solution, make inferences, visualize, ask and answer questions, make connections, make a prediction, and monitor comprehension.* However, LTELs cannot be expected to verbalize their predictions and inferences or visualize if they do not know 85 to 90 percent of the words necessary to understand the passage or to express the prediction/inference or to form mind-movies. This is where preteaching selected words comes in (Calderón 2007, 2018, 2019).

Moreover, LTELs might have difficulty making connections to certain prior knowledge that is not part of their culture or schooling experiences. Essentially, it is easier for LTELs to begin with *determining important information, summarization, asking and answering questions, finding evidence and monitoring comprehension.* High school teachers find that using think-alouds helps all students learn strategies for comprehending math, science, and social studies. LTELs need to apply a strategy immediately with a partner. This reinforces the knowledge of the strategy and gives teachers an opportunity to check the appropriate use of those strategies.

3. Partner Reading with Partner Summarization

Partner reading with frequent summarization was found to have even greater effect sizes for ELs than just partner reading by itself (Calderón, Hertz-Lazarowitz and Slavin 1998). Partners must be strategically selected. For instance, partner reading pairs can consist of a an LTEL and a student who is a more proficient reader. They read each paragraph in the parsed text, one student at a time, alternating sentences. They stop at the end of each paragraph to summarize verbally what they just read. The reason we want students to summarize verbally is because the more they articulate the information using the language from the paragraph, the more the brain consolidates language, literacy, and content. When instructing the students on how to do partner reading, the graph below can be used to inform the students about the process.

1. The teacher models with a student "reading by alternating sentences."

2. Partner A reads the first sentence.

3. Partner B reads the next sentence.

4. After each paragraph, partners verbally summarize what they read using as many Tier 2 and 3 words as possible.

5. Partners continue until they finish reading the section assigned.

Figure 5.8 Partner reading with summarization

Triad Reading and Triad Summarization

When there is a newcomer, or a student who needs a lot of help before reading with a partner, the triad reading will accelerate the learning to read for the three students. The newcomer/striving reader is placed in the middle of two proficient readers. One of the partners can be an LTEL who has gone through partner reading for some time and whose progress is quite evident. The newcomer/striving reader reads in a whisper along with partner one and then with partner two. This is called whisper reading. After a couple of weeks, the newcomer is reading better and is then assigned only one partner. Some newcomers and some LTELs may need some phonics instruction along with the regular classroom partner reading.

---

1. The newcomer (NC) is grouped together with two higher-level ELs or native English speakers (s1 and s2)
2. When s1 reads a sentence, NC whisper-reads the sentence.
3. When s2 reads a sentence, NC whisper reads along.
4. Eventually, the reading is done in this sequence:

$$s1 \rightarrow NC \rightarrow s2 \rightarrow NC \rightarrow s1 \rightarrow NC \rightarrow s2 \mid\rightarrow NC$$

5. This gives NC double turns during each cycle.

Figure 5.9 Partner Reading with a Newcomer (Triad Reading)

The summarization with a newcomer/striving reader also occurs in triads with the newcomer/striving reader restating what partner one said, and then repeating with partner two, until ready to summarize on her/his own. They continue in triads until the striving reader is comfortable to actively participate with only one partner.

---

1. The newcomer (NC) is grouped together with two higher-level ELs or native English speakers (s1 and s2)
2. When s1 summarizes, NC whispers the sentence or fragments or words.
3. When s2 summarizes, NC whispers the sentence or fragments or words.
4. Newcomer summarizes with a few cohesive sentences at the end:

$$s1 \rightarrow NC \rightarrow s2 \rightarrow NC \rightarrow s1 \rightarrow NC \rightarrow s2 \rightarrow NC$$

5. This gives NC double turns during each cycle.

Figure 5.10 Partner summarization with a newcomer (triad summarization)

SEL Competencies Learned during Reading

Doing partner reading is a golden opportunity to further expand the practice of SEL competencies. As with vocabulary, the social norms and shared agreements need to be taught, modeled, and reinforced every time students are working together. A quick reminder about everyone showing respect and support for one another is essential so that the students see that the teachers still believe that those SEL skills are important. The partner summarization with a newcomer or even with an LTEL is an extremely effective way for the stronger readers to show empathy and patience for the struggling reader as well as establish positive relationships. A classroom that focuses exclusively on academics loses out in educating the heart as well. For students who have not had positive experiences in a formal education setting, any intentionally planned activity that builds greater appreciation and understanding between students will have lasting positive effects on the EL and LTEL.

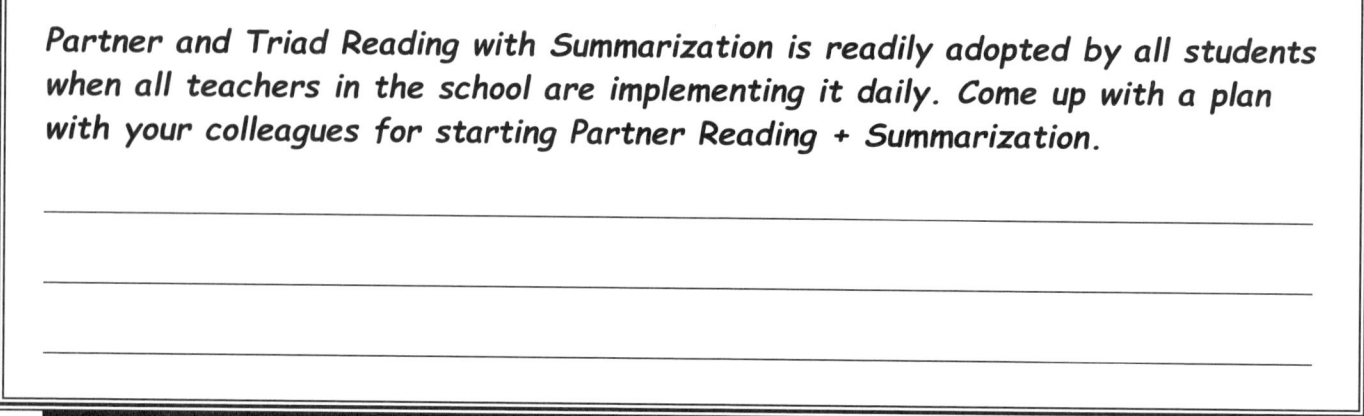

Partner and Triad Reading with Summarization is readily adopted by all students when all teachers in the school are implementing it daily. Come up with a plan with your colleagues for starting Partner Reading + Summarization.

Figure 5.11 Jot down your reflections to share later with your colleagues

4. Formulating Questions—Another Opportunity for Close Reading and Deep Learning

When testing the components of ExC-ELL™, we found that formulating questions is more challenging and exciting than just answering questions. After reading and summarizing verbally, the students can go back into the text to formulate questions instead of the traditional "answer these questions" approach. Writing a series of questions demonstrates students' ability to follow the details of what is explicitly stated in the text. When LTELs and all students have to formulate questions, they need to go back into the text, discuss their understanding and drafts. Did they use the academic language they have been learning, and work on grammatical features that hold quality questions together? Teachers keep in mind that writing high-quality text-dependent questions must be modeled. Begin with simple questions requiring attention to specific words, details, and arguments. Once students have practiced simple questions, they can move to higher level open-ended question formulation.

LTELs formulate and test the questions in teams of four. They write each question on a card with the answer on the back of the card, give themselves a team name, and hand it to the teacher. At www.calderonexc.com you can download cards for different levels of Bloom-type questions and a list of verbs and question stems for each level of Bloom.

Once the teacher has collected all the team cards, a cooperative learning activity called Numbered Heads Together is used to test the teams with one another's questions. This is a third time the students return to the text for *more close reading*. Now, they are looking for answers to the questions their peers have written.

---

1. Number off in your team from one to four.
2. Listen to the question your teacher reads.
3. Put your heads together and find the answer.
4. Make sure everyone in your team knows the answer.
5. Be prepared to answer when your number is called.
6. The team that wrote the question will be the judges/language monitors.
7. Use sentence starters, connectors, transition words...to add to others' answers.

Figure 5.12 Numbered Heads Together to Test Questions

Modeling Deep Learning

Deep learning combines knowledge of a subject and self-knowledge. Deep learning calls for using facts to analyze one's own feelings about those topics, forming thoughts and opinions, and connecting those thoughts and opinions with forward development of self and knowledge. When students are asked to find evidence or ways of refuting that evidence, they are forming an opinion based on that evidence. Those opinions and ideas become the basis for further questioning. Moreover, they serve as an anchor for further connections to the topic they are studying, defending, or refuting. LTELs will need visuals such as the following figure with an example of how to go from facts to opinions to forward thinking (Calderón, et al. 2017. Using the SEL framework, LTELs can also identify the skills/competencies they are applying as they go through this process. When it comes time to construct a narrative, remind them to reflect on their emotions as they recall some facts and examine their beliefs as they organize their claims.

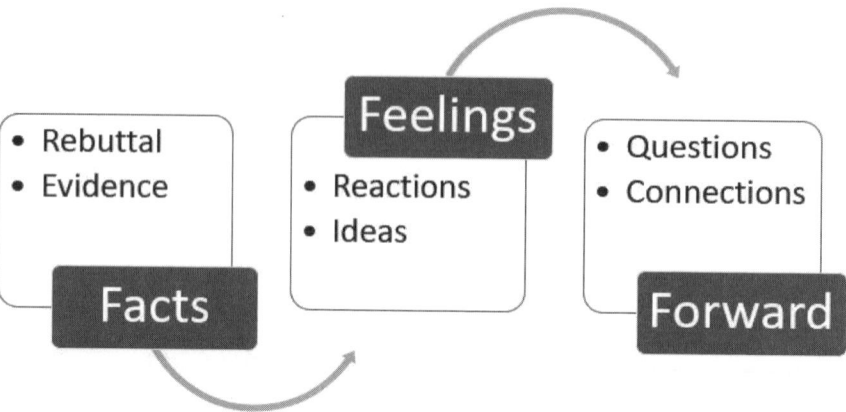

Figure 5.13 Deep learning with these strategies

Deep Learning occurs when students come to understand and make sense of important ideas, processes, and problem solving—and are able to transfer those understandings to new content and contexts. How does Formulating Questions help this deep learning of what they were reading?

_____

_____

_____

How does Numbered Heads Together help students go even deeper?

_____

_____

_____

Figure 5.14 Jot down your reflections to share later with your colleagues

SEL Competencies Developed through Question Formulation and Numbered Heads Together

The team that wrote the question becomes the "Language Monitors," listening carefully to the responses from the other teams. Language Monitors give feedback to the students from each team who were called to respond by reiterating the Tier 2 and 3 words they used in their answers, noting the connectors, transition, and sophisticated words. The respondents love to hear the positive feedback on their discourse. It also motivates them to be more and more prepared each time by using more sophisticated academic language. Can you imagine how students develop many more SEL skills during this activity?

Properly implemented, Numbered Heads Together has the profound effect of accelerating the learning and application of SEL skills to a new level. This is a powerful dynamic where achievement of the team is the goal, but individual accountability is a priority. Through this strategy, students learn the skills of collective responsibility, critical thinking skills, effective problem solving, and oral language development. This truly takes the learning and socialization to another level.

Discovering How Much Vocabulary They Learned

One follow-up strategy that confirms how much language students learned from reading, summarizing, formulating questions, and answering questions other teams wrote is called the Vocabulary Roundtable. In this strategy, students remain in teams of four. These are the instructions for the students for the two rounds.

---

1. Clear your desks.
2. Have only one piece of paper, but everyone needs a pencil.
3. Each student will write one key word or phrase and then pass the paper to the right.
4. Everyone must write a word or phrase.
5. Write a key word from the text and pass the paper.
6. Keep writing one word or phrase at a time until the teacher calls "stop" (after one minute). The words must be Tier 2 or 3.

Figure 5.15 Vocabulary roundtable—round one

After a minute, each team counts the words, and shares results. The teacher then informs that they have three minutes to re-read their text and learn more words in preparation for a second round. The instructions are as follows:

1. Put your heads together and come up with a strategy to improve your team total.
2. Reread/revisit the text for three minutes.
3. Learn more words.
4. Apply your strategy in Round 2 to try to get more words.
5. Follow the same rules as for Round 1.

Figure 5.16 Vocabulary roundtable—round two

After one minute, they count the words. The exciting outcome each time is that all teams improve their scores. They celebrate and enjoy the fact that they are improving their vocabulary, reading, and content knowledge exponentially.

SEL Competencies Developed through Round Table

From an SEL perspective, nothing is more exciting than having students work collaboratively on a competitive activity. There are multiple dimensions in this activity in which students can support one another, reinforce prior learning of vocabulary, and further develop SEL skills and competencies. By rating teams by their improvement rather than on overall competition against the scores of other teams, the LTEL should be liberated from feelings of shame and defeat and should rather build confidence that each student can learn from others and contribute to the overall success of the team. This empowers LTELs to want to participate more, knowing that they will be supported, included, and able to celebrate with their peers the immediate reward of accomplishment.

More Consolidation Strategies/Activities

There are several other strategies that students can do to reinforce their grammar, vocabulary, spelling, or comprehension. These can be done in pairs, triads, teams, or individually. Here are some suggestions for working in enrichment centers, or what are sometimes called stations. The same activities can be done virtually, on their own at first, and then compared/shared in Zoom breakout rooms.

Enrichment or Center Activities

In Pairs and Teams

- Discuss what they learned.
- Summarize what they have read so far.
- Practice formulating questions at different Bloom levels.
- Practice pronunciation and spelling of new words.
- Give each other spelling tests.
- Play word games.
- Take turns reading for fluency.

Self-Paced

- Complete word study assignments.
- Practice formulating questions.
- Read or re-read.
- Practice spelling.
- Practice pronunciation.
- Play word games.
- Write in journal.

The final wrap-up activity serves two purposes: (1) to debrief and find out what the students have learned about the content, language, reading, and themselves; (2) to celebrate small and large successes in a creative way that they self-select, such as writing a poem, a rap, or a role play. Students should have the option to create and share their voices in the closure activity.

Teaching the Strategies Virtually

The same instructional strategies that were described above for face-to-face or physical classrooms can be taught remotely. Creative teachers will also find ways to blend both and refine the delivery. We describe the way we present our interactive virtual workshops to train teachers and administrators on the twelve components.

The Virtual Lesson Components

Be it a virtual or physical classroom, twelve evidence-based empirically tested components (Figure 5.3) at the beginning of this chapter form the framework for comprehensive instruction and comprehensive professional development for the whole school. So far, we have described and given examples of components one through nine, as listed in this chapter. Chapter 6 will elaborate on writing.

The content of the twelve components is the same. There are only procedural adaptations that have been made. For example, the teacher can write out the objectives in a shared document and ask the students to keep them in their virtual folder where they will keep all the materials for that lesson. A slide with the text structure with Tier 2 words is also explained and given to them. For the Think Aloud, both teacher and students will need to see the text with the features being presented. A different text with many text features (for example, photos, illustrations, Quick Response codes (QR codes), bold print, italics, and quotation marks) can be given to the students to practice finding the text features.

The *Vocabulary 7 Steps* are presented by the teacher in the same way. However, the pair of students practice the sixth step in breakout rooms or with someone at home. They can also video their practice with the five or six words and share the video with a peer or the teacher. The important thing is that they receive feedback on their pronunciation and sentence-formation practice.

Partner Reading and Summarization can be taught the same way. After the teacher models with a student or shows a one-minute video, students practice with their buddy reading aloud, alternating sentences, and summarizing at the end of the paragraph in breakout rooms. The teacher can drop by to listen and redirect if necessary.

After reading, the teacher models how to construct the type of questions most appropriate for that unit. **The Student Formulated Questions** phase can take place in breakout rooms in teams of four (pairs are fine, too). The teacher prepares a shared online document ahead of time, which has a space for each team's name, their assigned level of Bloom's taxonomy, and space for their question. They give themselves a team name and it and their question and answer (or possible answers when it is an open-ended question) are shown to the teacher but not the rest of the students.

Once the teacher receives the students' questions, they proceed with the **Numbered Heads Together** activity as a whole group. The teacher reads a question to the whole group and states the name of the group. This group will be the language monitors for that question. They will take notes independently to record and remember words/language on which they want to give feedback to the students from the other teams as they are called to answer one by one. The language monitors give feedback. Each #2 student is expected to use connectors—transition words—to build upon the previous student's answer. The students should have the discourse cards or table tents (Figure 4.8 in chapter 4) with the transition, connectors, and sentence starters for this part.

Students remain in those teams to do the **Vocabulary Round Table** activity. The teacher provides them with another shared online document, where each student takes a turn quickly writing a word they remember from the text. For more structure, the teacher can have students write their names and their number at the top of the document—this will help them remember whose turn it is as they move quickly through the activity. After the first round, during the *"Learn More"* phase, the students remain in teams even though they are re-reading and learning more vocabulary on their own. They also discuss how to improve their score in the second round.

For all the strategies/activities, students can create a blog using Google Sites, Weebly, Word-Press, or another blogging platform to record thoughts or they can record videos on Flipgrid or create an online survey with Google Forms. Invent the graphic organizers you want your students to use and then store them.

Student Self-Assessment

Students, aware of their learning targets as they have been part of their formulation, are receiving, giving, and acting on concrete actionable feedback as part of the classroom's instructional assessment routine. These include establishing high expectations and clear goals with students coupled with student-led assessment (Gottlieb 2016). In the classroom, data are drawn from multiple sources, such as through observation, everyday activities, or long-term projects and in multimodal ways, that is through visual, graphic, digital, written, and/or oral means.

A final wrap-up activity in every lesson serves two purposes: (1) to debrief and find out what the students have learned about the content, language, reading, and themselves; and (2) to celebrate small and large successes in a creative way they self-select, such as writing a poem, a rap, or a role play. Students should have the option to create and share their voices in goals and assessments. Particularly under the COVID-19 ways we have had to adjust schooling.

- Shared learning goals and objectives with evidence to match
- Mutually agreed upon grading criteria
- Representation of multiple data source from multimedia products
- A balance of different types of assessments
- Student self-assessment and reflections

Figure 5.17 Students' Voice in Assessment

In addition to jointly developed rubrics and criteria, LTELs could record their learning progressions and/or thoughts about their academic growth. As they conference with their teachers, they can jot down main points about the conversation and their new insights. They can also keep track of which learning strategy works for them (learning how to learn). The following figures are used by students to record their learning.

Discussion 1:
Record your notes:

_____

_____

_____

Discussion 2:
Record your notes:

_____

_____

_____

Lessons learned so far:

_____

_____

_____

Figure 5.18 Students, record your thoughts

	Strategy	Describe	How did you use it?	What worked?	How can you improve?
1.					
2.					
3.					
4.					

Table 5.2 Student Debriefing Chart

A Caveat on Assessments

Reading programs and their assessments measure reading ability, which governs decisions regarding initial placement, selection of instructional programs, and reclassification. The goal of effective reading programs is to ensure that students attain reading proficiency that allows them to participate in more rigorous and academically challenging classes that prepare them for graduation and beyond. However, when these assessments or standardized testing is the sole source for accountability, it is often to the detriment of our diverse student populations. "It is only through a balanced assessment system that is learning-centered, taking place in everyday classroom activities and tasks, that we have a true sense of what students can do. Thus, schools need to endorse assessment as learning (student-driven) and assessment *for* learning (teachers facilitating students' actions) as companions to assessment of learning and as pathways to equity" (Zacarian, Calderón and Gottlieb 2021).

Conclusion

Reading has been overlooked for many years. Perhaps that is the reason why the country does not progress in the National Assessment of Educational Progress (NAEP) in reading, as compared to other countries. If reading has been troublesome for general education students, we can imagine it to be the same for LTELs. Nevertheless, we can change those trends. We can use the easy applicable reading and SEL strategies as combined here. They can be used virtually or in person or in hybrid

- Connect language, reading, and writing by having students collect interesting words in the text: polysemous words, cognates, and connectors/transition words. Show how they can use these in their Exit Pass at the end of class.

- Ask students to keep a digital journal containing reflections on their work: things that make them feel safe and happy, or anything they want. Encourage artwork, visuals, or charts.

- Keep the activities short and provide a time limit: ten minutes for Part 1).

- Give brief precise feedback immediately when possible. Otherwise, give students your feedback schedule (the last five minutes after . . . every Wednesday at . . .).

- Facilitate discussion and thinking using the social norm, "step in (as soon as your name is called), step out (quickly so that others step in), and hold your thought (when another is talking)," to ensure 100 percent participation.

- Facilitate informal time for their own chatter with friends or same language groups.

- Ask students to evaluate their own work as well as their peers' work, using, "Is there anything you might change?" or, "Can you explain it in a different way?" They can also use rubrics or narratives on Google Drive or Google Forms.

- Have a morning message to welcome students and add a motivational topic to discuss, such as what is happening in the community or in their own lives.

- Provide feedback in a quick email, highlighting a specific little task on an assignment that worked.

- Give LTELs choices of topics relevant to their daily realities and interests. If possible, have three lesson templates ready: high tech, low tech, and paper packets—for those who have more complete technology, those who only have a phone, and those who have no or limited technology.

- Engage in a range of multimodal texts: picture books, comics, slideshows, murals, posters, web pages, videos, emails, texting with memes, and using the language(s) they want to use.

- To meet the specific needs of your LTEL, offer choices of reading levels, complexity of materials, number of tasks addressed, and some extended time. Gently challenge them to move to another level after successfully completing each one.

Figure 5.19 Tips for supporting LTEL reading comprehension virtually and in person

Personal Reflections and Collegial Discussions

1. How are our LTELs doing in reading assessments?

   _____

   _____

   _____

2. Do they read every day with a buddy in every subject?

   _____

   _____

   _____

3. Do they summarize after each paragraph?

   _____

   _____

4. What else can we add to each lesson to ensure they learn comprehension skills?

   _____

   _____

   _____

5. How can ESLs and core content teachers work together on the development of reading skills?

   _____

   _____

   _____

Chapter 6

Writing to Expedite Learning for LTELs

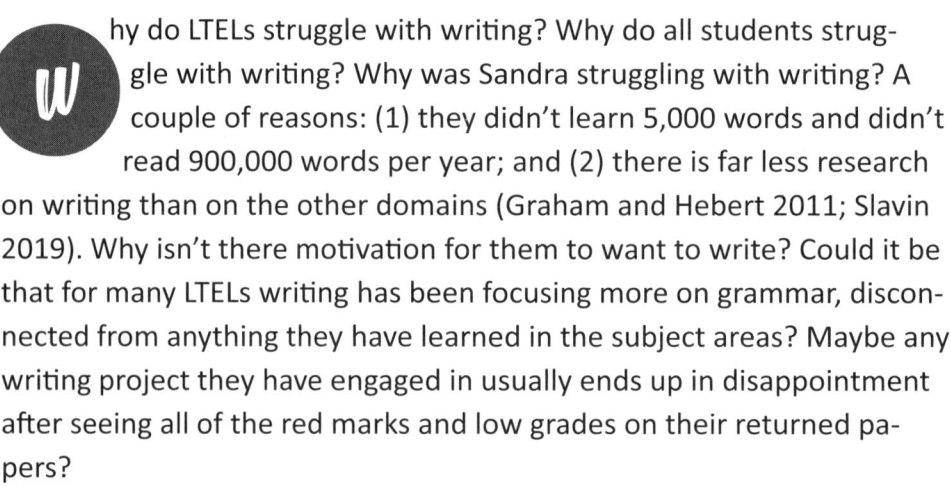

Why do LTELs struggle with writing? Why do all students struggle with writing? Why was Sandra struggling with writing? A couple of reasons: (1) they didn't learn 5,000 words and didn't read 900,000 words per year; and (2) there is far less research on writing than on the other domains (Graham and Hebert 2011; Slavin 2019). Why isn't there motivation for them to want to write? Could it be that for many LTELs writing has been focusing more on grammar, disconnected from anything they have learned in the subject areas? Maybe any writing project they have engaged in usually ends up in disappointment after seeing all of the red marks and low grades on their returned papers?

In elementary schools, ELs learn to write during language arts or ESL. In secondary schools, LTELs need to learn different types of writing for each subject area. Writing in math is different from writing personal narrative. Writing a comparison-contrasting composition for social studies is different from writing a poem. Science reports and business letters have different features.

For each core content subject, there are different language mechanics that go beyond a typical grammar lesson in language arts: sentence length, sentence structure, active/passive voice, first/third person, punctuation, spelling, and Tier 3 words. There are different text structures also: persuasive, argumentative, cause and effect, problem solving, essay, memoir, and descriptive. The author's purpose uses literary devices such as foreshadowing, nuance, ambiguity, analogy, conflict, characterization, dialog, citations, imagery, and sarcasm.

As adults, if we had to write using this variety of genre every week, wouldn't it be challenging? Can you imagine an LTEL having to use such a spectrum of techniques without being taught how to write in each subject area? Can you imagine how difficult writing can be for Sandra and other ELs when they have to work alone without any peer support, writing samples, and an empathetic ear to share their struggles and frustration.

There have been four benchmark meta studies and publications on writing, as follows:
- *Writing Next: Effective Strategies to Improve Writing of Adolescents in Middle and High Schools* (Graham and Perin 2007)
- *Writing to Read: Evidence for How Writing Can Improve Reading* (Graham and Hebert 2010)
- *Informing Writing: The Benefits of Formative Assessment* (Graham, Harris, and Hebert 2011)
- *A Quantitative Synthesis of Research on Writing Approaches in Grades 2nd—12th* (Slavin 2019)

The Universality Framework for Writing

Dr. Slavin's meta-analysis found programs that had positive effect sizes (ES=+16 to ES=+17) were the process writing model, cooperative learning, and programs integrating reading and writing. Based on the features that cut across these programs, and our previous five-year development and testing of the Bilingual Cooperative Integrated Reading and Composition (BCIRC), we put together the writing component of ExC-ELL™ that combines the writing process, cooperative learning (to develop SEL skills and master content), and integration of reading and writing.

In accordance with the extensive research on vocabulary, the findings from the Carnegie reports on adolescent literacy, the premises of the social emotional competencies, and the following research on writing, ExC-ELL™ has put together a universal framework for language, literacy, and content. ExC-ELL™ Universality Framework has been found to be applicable to all students, particularly disenfranchised Black and Latino students. Upon implementation, teachers immediately find that students from all cultural and linguistic backgrounds and all special needs and gifts as well as privileged students benefit from this framework. The writing component is based on the research described above, building upon specific strategies that we tested in highly diverse classrooms.

Premises for Teaching Writing in the Content Areas

- Establish writing routines that create a pleasant writing environment.
  - o This is what we have interpreted as a place to show empathy for the students and introduce SEL competencies as students work in teams for writing.

- o Social norms and shared agreements need to be developed and agreed to by all students so that they understand the reasons for the norms and make a personal commitment to practice them during every peer and adult interaction.
- Implement a process approach to writing.
  - o The writing process gives LTEL an extended opportunity to discuss, probe, and ponder before they write. In teams they learn to draft, revise, edit, and publish compositions.
- Write stems from reading models.
  - o After preteaching vocabulary to comprehend a mentor text, LTEL can use the language and sentence models from the text they read to produce higher quality writing.
- Create routines for students to write expository text frequently.
  - o LTEL and all students need to write in all subject areas to practice different genres.
  - o Core content can easily be integrated into creative writing as well.
- Design instructional routines in which students work together.
  - o Integrate Cooperative Learning and ample peer discourse throughout the sequence of the writing process.
  - o Relationship building during cooperative learning exercises should be a high priority along with academics and teachers ensuring that students have had plenty of practice in the SEL competencies before engaging in the activities.
  - o Cooperative Learning activities have to be well thought out and planned in a way that allows students to practice social skills, valuing a diversity of perspectives, being ready to use restorative practices in the event that a conflict should arise.
- Establish goals for students' writing.
  - o We set high expectations and expect students to learn how to edit, revise, and submit creative compositions by using criteria such as: use persuasive or argumentative language, comparing or contrasting with the support of evidence; use Tier 2 words to connect sentences.
  - o Remind students of the qualities of a growth mindset that focuses on students' strengths, potential and beliefs that we learn best when we take risks and make mistakes, embrace challenges, persist in the face of setbacks and find lessons and inspiration in other people's success.
- Establish programs that teach students to assess their own drafts and give/get feedback.
  - o We integrate Ratiocination, Cut & Grow, Powerful Conclusions and powerful Titles. Students learn routines, norms, and rubrics for peer feedback.
  - o Embedded in the program is explicit practice of embracing feedback, criticism, and self-assessment so that they can "train their brain" to think critically and pursue a problem-solving mindset rather than a defeatist attitude and giving up.
- Create programs that provide extensive professional development to teachers, in which they experience the strategies they will employ.
  - o Our comprehensive face-to-face or virtual professional development includes model-

ing, practice, feedback, and coaching for teachers and administrators who will build support for quality implementation.

o   The final step is to help build each strategy into each teacher's lesson plan. A lesson template is provided. (Download the lesson template from www.calderonexc.com).

The Strategies and Components for Writing

Writing Addresses Equity, Culture, and Diversity

As you plan for writing instruction, think about writing as the perfect vehicle to capture students' voices, especially those of LTEL and Black students' voices that perhaps do not have as many opportunities to express themselves. Students' lives are already a great topic for writing. Help them to connect their histories and emotions to what they are studying and having to write about. Another way to help them connect to their culture is to encourage them to use art, songs, poetry, and monologue as complementary tools to their project-based or Science, Technology, Engineering, the Arts and Mathematics (STEAM) writing assignments.

Create writing assignments to develop knowledge and skills to solve problems of the community or society in general. Help them to further develop that social conscience that has been dormant in many of our young people these past few years as they repress the injustices they have seen or encountered in schools and society (Jagers, Rivas-Drake and Borowski 2018). When writing about literature, show them how to probe deeper into the motives and feelings of characters. Use different types of writing in literature (poetry, haiku, skits, own characters, humor, satire). For writing in social studies or historical events, ask them to build on their opinions about diversity, discrimination, and implications for today's issues. In science, help them to see how science can improve people's lives and to recognize our responsibility within the different branches of science. These student-meaningful approaches are more likely to generate their interest in writing (see examples with Role, Audience, Format, Topic (RAFT) and STEAM below).

LTEL Want to Be Involved in Decisions

Ask students to help you create a climate for cooperative writing where everyone practices empathy and uses cooperative learning norms to guide their learning about academic writing. Offer consistent support for working through learning difficulties. Regularly, ask for feedback from students when you conference one-on-one. Provide as much voice and choice as possible. Sandra has developed many skills and talents outside of school. She likes to draw maps and label them in Spanish for her parents and siblings of where they need to go in the city. She loves geography and history and is now interested in place names in her city. After her peers found out about her geography knowledge, they started asking her to join a team. Thus, these new relationships and her special skills could begin to lead to in-depth learning if we provide opportunities to investigate topics through interest-based inquiry or project-based learning or cross-disciplinary connections. We recommend focusing on the big ideas and key concepts of your own discipline and ask LTEL for ideas they are most interested in exploring.

More inquiry/project-based learning, integrated learning, cooperation, critical thinking, and problem solving through student-centered collaborative structures allow for creativity, excitement, self-assessment, and team assessment.

Figure 6.1 Creating creativity, excitement, and assessment

Remember That Before Writing . . .

. . . the teacher has taught components 1 through 9 of the 12 components. Hence, the LTEL have learned five words before reading, learned many more words while doing Partner Reading, and learned how to put those words into discourse during Partner Summarization after every paragraph. Subsequently, they went back into the text to formulate questions and learned more words, sentence structures, and more content. Finally, they mastered more words during two rounds of Vocabulary Round Table. With all this language, syntax, and content, the LTEL and low-performing writers are ready to write (unless some of those critical steps were skipped). The end product will show the difference between doing all nine components before they start writing versus skipping some of the nine pre-writing components.

Forming Partnerships and Teams

With all the changes students have had to endure this year, positive relationships will be most welcomed by all students. Teacher skill at dividing students into pairs or teams of three or four is now a critical SEL process. Just as with the 6th step in teaching vocabulary and with partner reading, the assembling of compatible teams cannot be left to chance nor does the practice of self-selecting work for all students. Building good relationships between teachers and students and between students and students is dependent on teachers making critical and proactive decisions that are in the best interest for ELs as well as for high achievers. Building trust is just as important as teaching content.

Build peer interaction in every phase: Prewriting > Drafting > Editing > Revising > Final Editing > Sharing

Figure 6.2 Collaborative writing process for Project-Based Learning

Whatever their writing assignment, it starts with a draft. This collaborative draft will proceed with peer assistance for revision and editing. When all writers work in teams of three or four, their synergy enhances the quality and quantity of writing. Here is how we can guide students through the process for academic writing.

Before Students Write

Begin by explaining the standard, assessment rubrics and the purpose/focus for this writing project. Distribute Table Tents to have on hand as their writing progresses. Here are two examples of what can go on a Table Tent or a shared online document or virtual bulletin board. Recommend they find a place where they can keep these handy, since they will be using them frequently. They might want to place them where their Tier 2 transitions and connectors are saved and any Tier 3 words they will need to use repeatedly, and a couple of Tier 1 words that they frequently forget how to spell.

Text Type	Purpose
Arguments or persuasive writing: building arguments, writing argument essays, problem-solution essay, editorial, public-service announcement, response to a scientific responsive prompt	To change the reader's thinking, move the reader to action, or convince the reader to accept the writer's explanation of a problem or concept by supporting claims with clear reasons and relevant evidence
Informative: Explanatory Writing: process essay, definition essay, comparison-contrast essay, cause-effect essay, response to a scientific explanatory prompt	To examine a topic and convey ideas, concepts, and information through the selection, organization, and analysis of relevant content in order to increase knowledge, explain a procedure, or explore a concept in depth
Narratives	To entertain, instruct, or inform by developing real or imagined experiences or events using effective techniques, relevant descriptive details, and well-structured event sequences
Personal Writing	Journal writing, using learning logs, writing blog posts, emails, tweets
Research Writing	Summarizing, paraphrasing and quoting, writing research reports

Source: Adapted from Calderón 2020.

Table 6.2 Purpose of writing

Text Structure	Purpose
Problem/Solution	Show the development of a problem and one or more solutions to the problem. The author states a problem and various solutions or uses a question-answer format and addresses the problem.
Compare/Contrast	Point out likenesses (comparison) and/or differences (contrast) among facts, people, events, or concepts.
Cause/Effect	Show how facts, events, or concepts (effects) happen or come into being because of other facts, events, or concepts.
Description	Address a specific topic and its attributes. Provide main idea(s) supported by rich/descriptive details.
Sequence	Provide information/events in chronological order. Present details in specific order to convey specific meaning.

The Writing Process in Physical Classroom Interactions

We have learned through several years of testing instructional methods in hundreds of classrooms which approach to the writing process yields greater benefits for Newcomers and LTEL in particular. The process described in the following pages is the same now being implemented virtually. We begin with the in-person description for schools that still have that option, and then describe the adaptations of all these features and activities as they can be used in the virtual approach.

Drafting

Now that students have language and content stored in their brains, they can work with peers to draft the first copy. Teams of three or four work best, especially since they have had multiple opportunities to practice their SEL competencies before engaging in this activity. Some social norms can be:

- Everyone contributes,
- No one passes a turn but can repeat a sentence.
- Try not to keep others waiting too long.
- Be polite.
- Stay on task,
- Other norms that fit behaviors you want or do not want to see.

The Write-Around strategy serves to engage the students in a safe environment to get ideas on paper. Students know that there is an editing and revising stage where they can fix spelling or grammar, add more evidence or more sophisticated language. For now, the goal is to get the content ideas out. If necessary, they can go back into the text to scan for content before they start the draft. Moreover, they can use a graphic organizer to connect that content to their own views or creative thoughts. The steps of the first written draft are as follows.

Write-Around Part 1

- Students work in teams of 3 or 4.
- Students agree to follow the shared agreements for effective collaboration.
- Students clear their desks.
- Each student has one piece of paper and a single pen or pencil.
- Each student writes down the sentence starter, and then completes a sentence.
- After completing the sentence, each student passes the paper to the person to the right.
- The student receiving the paper reads what is written, adds a sentence, and passes the paper to the right.
- The process continues until the teacher calls time (after about 12 minutes or a full page of writing).

For drafting, the teacher can give the teams a sentence stem to get them started writing. For example:

Global warming has become controversial due to . . .

Once they complete the sentence prompt, they pass the paper to the right. They are asked to use as many Tier 2 and 3 words as they can. It usually takes twelve or so minutes for the pairs or teams to complete three-quarters of a page or a full page. You will want that much writing in order to have enough material to edit and revise.

Write-Around Part 2

- Students take turns doing a Read-Around-Aloud.
- They read the composition each is holding to the team.
- They can choose one to revise and edit as a team or work on the team composition they are holding.

We emphasized again that the teams for the Write-Around phrases must be strategically selected and arranged. Students may self-select on certain occasions, but these teams need to have an even balance of the different levels of English proficiency to make the activity more inclusive, equitable, and successful. Otherwise, with self-select practices students will naturally gravitate toward their friends and/or intentionally exclude others who they perceive may bring their scores down. We want the LTELs to feel excluded, ignored, or even ridiculed because of the negative perception that they lack intelligence because of language ability. Interestingly, even those students who silently or vociferously oppose inclusion soon find that the LTEL has talents that enhance a team product.

Initially, during the Write-Around activity, ELs and LTELs should be allowed to copy what the other students have written if they are struggling to think of what to say or how to say it. This gets them actively engaged in the writing process from day one, builds confidence in doing the activity and teaches the other students the skills of patience, respect, and compassion. For LTEL this process helps in overcoming negative experiences and building trust in their classmates and in the writing process.

First Edit/Revision with Ratiocination

During the drafting, the teacher is gently milling around monitoring the teams' writing to see where they might need extra help. During the Ratiocination, the teacher asks the students to check their papers for a particular purpose, such as overuse of some words or repeated words at the beginning of a sentence or some pattern that needs to be fixed.

Afterwards, the teacher may need to do a mini lesson before the students check for a particular element of grammar. Thereafter, each time students are assigned a writing task, the teacher starts by checking for one feature from the examples in the graphic below. The editing strategies build incrementally as weeks go by and students add more strategies. **You can find more Table Tents at** www.exc-ell.com.

> ***Ratiocination: A Systematic Approach to Editing/Revision:*** *a logical, step-by-step process to circle, underline, square, color-code, analyze, evaluate, and rework your writing.*

Figure 6.3 Definition of ratiocination

Through Ratiocination, teachers teach students to apply specific skills in context. The teacher guides students to focus on the use of specific elements of language. However, the students are responsible for checking their own papers, thus reducing the paper load for the teacher. Most important, students are responsible for identifying elements that need to be changed or improved. They become mindful of their own repeated miscues and consciously try to avoid them, thereafter. During the phases of writing, students are also learning to cooperate, offer assistance, accept assistance, and become self-directed.

Teachers need to explicitly demonstrate and model both the strategy of Ratiocination and the SEL competencies that will be observed before students start to write. After that, ask students to apply Ratiocination only on items that they have practiced and learned. While they are working on a draft, if you notice certain patterns across the board that need to be fixed, conduct a mini lesson before they apply or go back for a second round of Ratiocination. For example, if you observed that the students have a problem with initial words for starting a sentence, teach a mini lesson on sentence connectors/transition words and phrases before asking students to draw a rectangle around each verb. The whole team works together to correct.

For Ratiocination, students will need colored markers or crayons to circle, box, or highlight the features called for. For instance, they can box the first word/phrases of every sentence with green. Then, they make a list of the boxed words/phrases. This will immediately flag repetition of words such as "the," "they," and "also," or the use of "unwanted words" at the beginning of a sentence such as "and," "because," and "like." Always look for the prevalence of grammar or spelling errors and assign those for one of the Ratiocination activities.

Virtual	In-Person	Task
Italicize	Box	Box the first word (or Tier 2 phrase) in every sentence. Decide to keep or change to a sophisticated transition word or connector. Make a list of first words/phrases.
Bold	Circle	Punctuation, dubious spelling, grammar (tense, passive voice or lack of), "to be" verbs—is, am, are, was, were, be, being, been—are they correctly used? Decide to keep or change to an active verb.
Underline	Underline Tier 1 words	Find Tier 1 words. Decide: keep or substitute with Tier 2 word.
Highlight alternating sentences	Highlight alternating sentences	Highlight alternating sentences using two different colors to show the variety of sentence length.
Differentiation or individualized	Differentiation or Individualized	Student-centered differentiation. What does Margarita need to work on? How about Daniel? Later, let the LTEL choose the item to Ratiocinate.

Table 6.3 Ratiocination

Revising: Cut & Grow

After the initial editing with Ratiocination, students will also become aware of sentences that need elaboration or evidence from the text. They can use the revision strategy called Cut & Grow for that purpose.

Process for Cut & Grow

- Students find a sentence that needs elaboration: evidence, claim, or counterclaim.
- Students cut their compositions right after the sentence where they are going to add evidence from the text.
- The additional sentence(s) are written on the colored sheet. Once written, the students tape the rest of their composition onto the colored sheet.
- Students re-read their improved compositions.

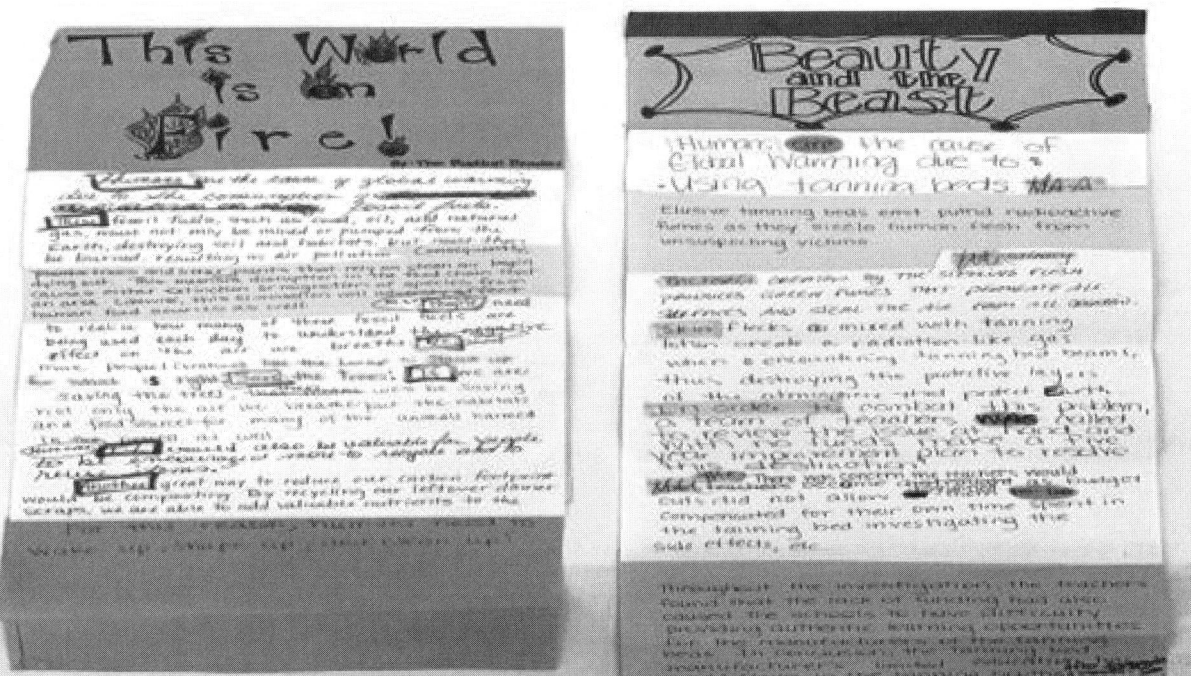

Figure 6.4 Cut & Grow samples (Calderón 2018)

This step is essential in helping LTELs develop their critical thinking skills by evaluating their work and reflecting on how they can add more of their personal experiences and culture in the text. For example, knowing that this is an ongoing process, LTELs will begin to feel more comfortable in reflecting on additional dimensions of their history, opinions, and emotions in conveying a specific point or message, especially after experiencing social separation from their peers for an extended period of time, health-related encounters, as well as the traumatic experience of dealing with the scarcity of essential survival resources at home or worse.

More Editing

Students can come back to Ratiocination to edit their papers. They can go back and code:

- Spelling
- Punctuation
- Simple sentences to change into compound sentences
- Statements that need support in the form of:
    o   evidence
    o   detail
    o   citations or references

Write-Around Part 3 – Final Editing and Refining

For the final refining stage, the students can review the following list and select the suggestion that best fits their final sweep. You can ask them to do the following:

- Edit/Revise the introduction to present your claim/thesis and/or to hook the reader.
- Add more Tier 2 & 3 words.
- Edit/Revise the evidence, explanations, and examples to provide strong support for the claim/ counterclaim. Present support in logical order.
- Introduce the claim(s), acknowledge alternative claims, and organize the reasons and evidence clearly.
- Support the claim(s) with clear reasons, examples, and relevant credible evidence.
- Use words and phrases/transitions to clarify the relationships among claims, reasons, and evidence.

- Establish and maintain a formal style.
- Provide a concluding statement or section that follows from and supports the argument presented.

Powerful Conclusions and Titles

Once the students agree that the draft is ready for the teacher, they finish with the following steps by

- Adding a powerful ending or conclusion.
- Giving it a title—an attention grabber
- Selecting a reader to share with the class
- Preparing the volunteer to read it to the class with fluency, prosody, and enthusiasm

Using the Writing Process Virtually

All stages of the Write-Around can be done virtually. We provided straightforward explanation so that a teacher can provide the information on their screen, showing each stage. After a teacher explanation of the process, students can work in teams of three or four in breakout rooms using a shared online document to compose their draft. You might want to post these instructions:

- You will both write at the same time. Partner A will write the first sentence in their essay while Partner B writes the first sentence on their own.
- Then it gets interesting. *Switch* essays, so that Partner A writes the second sentence in Partner B's essay, and vice versa.
- Continue *switching*, so that each follows the pattern.
- Continue writing until time is up.

Figure 6.5 Instructions for drafting in breakout rooms

A video of the drafting process will help clarify that part. You can go to www.exc-ell.com for a video. Pictures of examples can also be shown for each stage. As you teach this strategy, we recommend that you video each stage so you can share with other classes or give access to LTELs who need to review.

Some teachers ask the students to use different color fonts as they draft the shared document. This way it is easier to keep track of who is writing. In the final stage, all colors are turned into black because by then all students have contributed, and it becomes a team product.

In the breakout room they will edit their essay using the Ratiocination chart. Both partners will work together to edit essay number one.

In the second phase, Ratiocination, ask them to go back into their breakout room and work with their partner to do their first edit. Afterwards, they are ready to cut and grow the essay together. They choose one or two sentences in the essay that need elaboration, evidence, claim, or counterclaim, and add to it.

At various intervals bring the teams together to debrief by asking: How did it go?

Do you have any questions? Once the product is finished, a volunteer reads it online to the whole class. They can video the reading ahead of time if they are shy about reading in public.

Ask students to keep a virtual journal containing reflections on their work. Once in a while, they can also write about things that make them feel safe and happy, or anything they want. Encourage artwork, visuals, or charts. Offer Tier 2 words, sentence stems, and paragraph frames. Give LTEL choices of topics relevant to their daily realities and interests. Provide timely and individualized feedback. Have students email or text their written work.

Applying the Writing Process to Other Writing Assignments

The process for team or partner Drafting, Ratiocination, Cut & Grow, Powerful Conclusions, and Powerful Titles can be used for other types of writing. The more they apply the strategies across the board, the faster their writing improves. Include other types of writing such as:

- ✔ Independent writing such as Exit Slips and summaries
- ✔ RAFT products—Role, Audience, Format, Topic
- ✔ Fiction—short stories, poetry, songs
- ✔ Non-fiction—biographies, own histories

RAFT

RAFT gives students the opportunity to consider a topic from different perspectives. It focuses on an assignment that offers students a fresh and creative way to think about writing while enhancing understanding of a unit of study or a topic. Following a unit of study, the teacher creates a variety of RAFT writing tasks. The teacher assigns a writing experience to each student or pairs. One requirement is that they use Ratiocination and Cut & Grow and submit that draft along with the final product. LTEL benefit from working with a partner to learn the strategies. They learn self-reflection from peers and teacher feedback, which can be applied independently later on.

- R = role (Who are you as a writer?) —Allows students to take on a variety of roles to explore different points of view.
- A = audience (To whom are you writing?)—The audience is clearly defined.
- F = format (What form will the writing take?)—Essay, speech, letter, dialog, memo, and so on.
- T = topic (What is the subject?)—Must be narrow enough so students are not overwhelmed

Figure 6.6 RAFT

R	A	F	T
News reporter	College-educated adults	News article	Global warming
Astronomer	First graders	Travel guide	Journey through the Solar System
Acute triangle	Obtuse triangle	Letter	Differences among triangles
Jackie Robinson	Hall of Frame audience	Acceptance speech	My life in baseball
Tornado tracker	Weather reporter	Interview	Facts about tornados
Hermione Granger	Harry Potter	Dialog	Why are you so suspicious?
Rosa Parks	Historians	Diary entry	The boycott

Figure 6.7 RAFT

RAFT gives students many options to be creative and enjoy creating an original piece. They can write poetry, letters, biographies, songs, plays, theater productions, television productions, cartoons, podcasts, fliers, or any creative format they can come up with. This is also a great opportunity for students to choose who they want to work with. Latinx can work with other Latinx to inspire a collective cultural masterpiece. Black students can work on formats of their choice. Notwithstanding, most of the collaborative work ought to be inclusive in order to avoid discriminatory practices and to build cultural acceptance and respect.

Narratives

Narratives focus on developing real or imagined experiences or events using effective techniques, relevant descriptive details, and well-structured event sequences. For this, the writer must:

- Establish a context, introduce a narrator or characters, and organize an event sequence.
- Employ narrative techniques such as dialog, pacing, description, and reflection to develop experiences, events, and/or characters.
- Use a variety of transition words and punctuation features to convey sequence and signal shifts.
- Use precise words and phrases, relevant descriptive details, and sensory language.
- Provide a conclusion that reflects on the narrated experiences or events.
- Provide a story map to guide the narrative. Include Beginning (characters, setting, problem/conflict); Middle (what events happened); End (how the problem or conflict was resolved). (adopted from Calderón, et al. 2010)

Rip-n'-Rite

This is another creative and fun way of using all the drafting, editing, and revising strategies students have learned in the writing process. Now they apply them to Rip-n'-Rite! It works best in face-to-face teams, but also virtually. We hope some creative teachers will take on the challenge of developing a creative virtual process and share with us.

The purpose is to develop narratives that combine several criteria. For example, students must use

- Narrative—setting, character, plot, problem-solution, denouement, surprise ending, or other creative author crafts
- Dialogue or argumentative discourse
- Tier 2 or Tier 3 words and box each ("initially," "additionally," "following," "after," "not long after," "afterward," etc.)

- Each student rips a sheet of different-colored construction paper into creative pieces.
- Share your piece with your team and talk about it—what does it look like?
- Design a team story with plot, characters, setting, and dialog.
- Paste the pieces of the story on a chart paper, online document, or other place to share later.
- Share your story with the class.

Figure 6.8 Designing a story

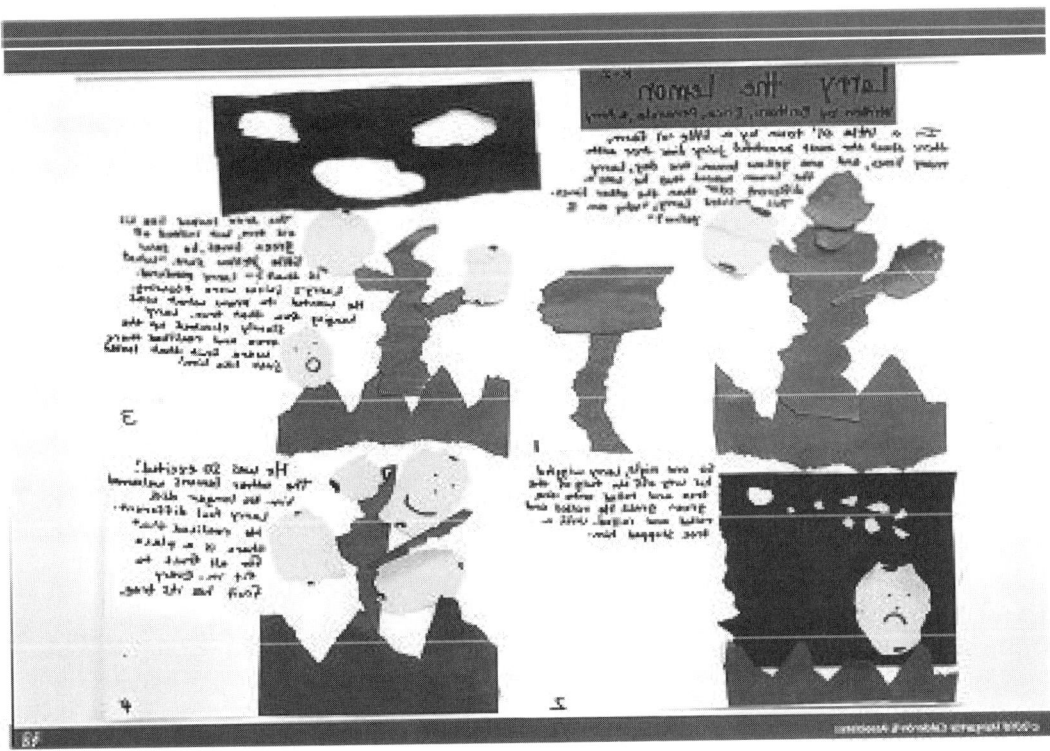

Figure 6.9 Rip-n'-Rite example

Mini Lessons

Mini lessons are necessary for some or all students to master specific elements of writing. Mini lessons are ways of differentiating instruction. Whereas Newcomers need basic noun–verb–object, the LTELs need combining sentences or to use imagery. The lessons should be short, ten minutes or so, and focus on one aspect of the writing they are about to begin, or are engaged in. The lessons can be delivered one-on-one, in a small group, or to the whole class. Topics include what students need: subject–verb agreement, transitions, dialog, combining sentences, etc.

A fun end-of-a-unit activity is giving students voice and choice again to use a preferred medium of summarizing what they learned and how they feel about it. The following consolidation activity generates amazing creativity and joy in presenting to the class.

> Write a jingle, rap, poem, or flyer that reflects what you have learned *about writing*.
> You can use music, dance, or movement.
> It should take seven minutes to prepare.
> It should take three minutes to present.
> Involve your whole team!

Figure 6.10 Team consolidation and debriefing

More Communication—Creative Communication

Creative thinking-writing means using Creative Communication—free talk about topics students want to discuss before writing. Students can build up ideas by extensive talk with peers. They only need some guidelines in the form of bullets that can be placed on Table Tents such as the following.

Take five or ten minutes to talk to your partner to
- clarify or support ideas, a concept, a term
- edit or elaborate a sentence
- fill information gaps
- discuss, interpret character traits
- look up more information
- find and discuss statistics
- look for or draft claims or counterclaims, basic principles, opinions, beliefs, relationships, themes

Source: Adapted from: Calderón 2020.

Figure 6.11 Table tent for creative writing communication

As we move into the actual writing activity it must be kept in mind that this is not purely a mechanical process to produce a final writing product. Ultimately, the process is just as important as the final product. This is a wonderful opportunity for teachers to continue to refine their language, reading comprehension, and SEL skills while facilitating the writing process.

Progress monitoring and formative assessments is the gathering of data for the purpose of making instantaneous and timely decisions, whether or not to intervene or allow students to make grammatical mistakes while in a highly productive and creative mode, whether or not to guide individual students or teams through the process as needed or to pause the entire class to make a point that might not apply to all. These are considerations for adults to make in the context of enhancing their own SEL skill set and sensitivity.

Reaching higher levels of interdependency while empowering independent readers and writers is the ultimate goal as we focus on the integration of SEL, language, and literacy. This is at the heart of Responsible Decision Making—making ethical, constructive choices about personal and social behavior that considers the well-being of self and others and problem-solving effectively while being respectful of people similar to and different from oneself.

The Benefits of Formative Assessment during Uncertain Times

We often hear "Maslow before Bloom" but Tom Gusky and Peter DeWitt agree that we should pay attention to both. We can be empathetic on the side of rigor and assessment. The purpose of assessments is to give students feedback on their performance. It is to help them see where they can improve. We can even ask an LTEL, "Tell me, how would you like to show what you have learned so far? Would you like to make a video and show me? How else can you show?"

Another question teachers keep asking Gusky—Is it OK to offer retakes? Can students, particularly the ones who did not have access to technology in the spring, retake tests as they continue trying to catch up? The answer is "of course" as long as there are corrective activities in between. Take, for example, the Vocabulary Round Table; we built in a very important corrective activity between the two rounds. In that structured hiatus, the students get a chance to go back into the text and learn more words. They also get to discuss and plan with their peers how to improve their score on the second round. During that discussion they are applying decision-making, negotiating, suspending opinions, reaching consensus, showing respect, offering assistance, and taking the initiative to include LTEL in the activities to name a few. This is the type of corrective activity that can be built wherever the students show a need to retake a test, redo a paper, or reach a goal.

Final Team and Self-Evaluation

Students need to know how well they did in identifying and coalescing important information into a meaningful learning experience. They need to know how well they accomplished their task, how well they used the learning strategies, and what they would do to improve next time.

On a scale of one to three, how well did you do? Which essential item did you use?			
Essentials for Excellent Writing	Team	Myself	Next Steps for Improvement
Difficult vocabulary words and in-text definitions			
Main ideas/arguments and related Supporting ideas/evidence			
Headings, transitional, and other Tier 2 words and phrases			
Illustrations graphs, art, other signposts			
Other difficult words (non-science vocabulary) and sentence construction			
Words for making inferences			
Words for making conclusions			

Table 6.4 Rubrics to gauge student performance (Calderón 2018)

Cooperative/Collaborative Writing Online

Teachers have found ways to do team writing online using a variety of tools. They share the screen to model and give the instructions or post key vocabulary. Teachers like to use breakout rooms to form teams randomly but making sure that the ELs are distributed among all teams. This gives ELs more exposure to and engagement with English. Albeit, once in a while teams with a common first language can be encouraged to write in that language. Pride in one's home language is sustained with writing.

Each team in the breakout rooms discusses the content they just read before they begin to do a draft. It is easy for the teacher to jump in and listen to each team as they map out their draft. They do their Write-Around by saying one sentence at a time and writing it on a digital whiteboard or shared document. For the editing, they have ample discussions, again using the Ratiocination chart. Afterwards, they can do a Cut & Grow online by actually cutting out a sentence or adding to sentences in their text. Teachers find that, with this process, all students are more engaged and more excited to "get it right."

To continue building on the writing skills developed during team writing, teachers may find journaling to be one of the most effective tools to reinforce and support the ongoing process of ELs improving their writing. Journaling can be an informal way for students to record their ideas and feelings after a particular team writing or a teacher's mini lesson. This could include writing about upcoming assignments, expectations in preparation for a trip, to learn how to make a list of important tasks to do or to express themselves through a personal and creative outlet. "Journaling has the added benefit of improving self-awareness and self-management, while providing a foundation for social-awareness, relationship skills, and responsible decision making" (Merrow 2019).

Cooperative/Collaborative Writing in the Computer Room or with Tablets

Students can pull their desks together in quads or triads or even in straight lines as some computer rooms have been set up. With tablets on their desks, they can write a sentence and pass the tablet to the right for the next student to add a sentence. With computers in a straight line, the students move from one computer to the next for several rounds.

Just as in paper and pencil or online, the tablets and computers can make writing exciting by using the same routines and constant back and forth discussions with peers.

Conclusion

As with vocabulary and reading, writing is just as much as an academic exercise as it is social and emotional. Teaming strategies that focused on building relationships makes writing much easier and attainable for ELs. As we saw with Sandra, associating writing with social interactions with other students with whom they have built trust and a positive relationship is essential to prepare ELs to write with greater ease and fluency. As with reading, ELs are also practicing the competencies of Self-Management, Social Awareness and Relationship Skills. Honoring and building on students' intrinsic motivation will lead to engagement and achievement. We have seen that with these writing strategies ELs can associate classroom learning experiences around having the opportunity to construct knowledge and co-create a writing product through a collaborative and cooperative process that is safe and motivating. Research shows that writing in the classroom can help students in setting and achieving goals, boosting memory and comprehension, improving communication skills, and providing organization practice, leading to a reduction in stress (Pennebaker 2004). For LTELs and their peers it is also a means to develop empathy and equity in every classroom.

Personal Reflections and Collegial Discussions

1. How are our LTELs doing in reading assessments?

    _____

    _____

    _____

2. Do they read every day with a buddy in every subject?

    _____

    _____

    _____

3. Do they summarize after each paragraph?

    _____

    _____

    _____

4. What else can we add to each lesson to ensure they learn comprehension skills?

    _____

    _____

    _____

5. How can ESLs and core content teachers work together on the development of reading skills?

    _____

    _____

    _____

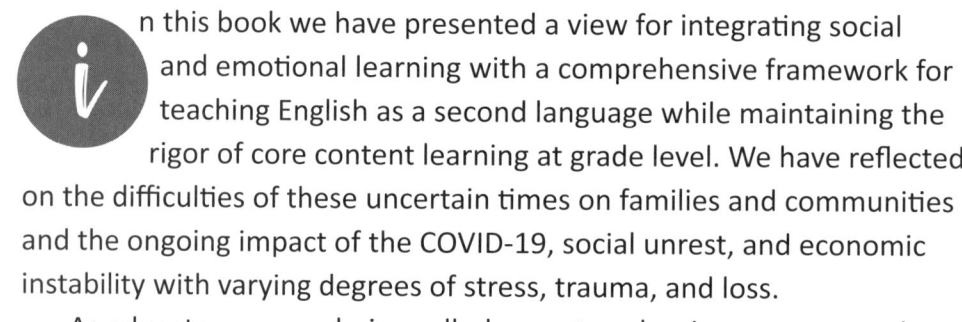

Chapter 7

Integrating SEL and LTEL Instruction

in this book we have presented a view for integrating social and emotional learning with a comprehensive framework for teaching English as a second language while maintaining the rigor of core content learning at grade level. We have reflected on the difficulties of these uncertain times on families and communities and the ongoing impact of the COVID-19, social unrest, and economic instability with varying degrees of stress, trauma, and loss.

As educators we are being called upon to usher in a new era and dimension of education that requires a new level of thinking, interacting, relating, and preparing our students for a different society. Under these circumstances, a greater focus on social and emotional learning must be embedded into every aspect of instruction and social interaction, ensuring that equity, inclusion, and collaborative practices are embedded within our thinking and ensuring that the most vulnerable of our students are not left behind. Transforming our traditional way of thinking about the diversity in our schools is foundational to transforming how we relate to children and their families, how we define accountability, and how we prepare our materials and resources to support the desired outcomes for all children.

Relational practices such as teambuilding activities, welcoming routines, shared agreements, and embedding SEL skills in every lesson and assignment should be seen as essential for student success. When included in the very essence and core of the learning experience for ELs and LTELs it is a matter of time before SEL competencies become the bedrock of a classroom and school culture resulting in greater academic gains, graduation rates, and productive and contributing members of a community. We have seen that, in their absence, ELs are more at risk of becoming LTELs, creating an ongoing narrative of systemic and structural practices that have produced less than desirable results. The impact is long term, economically devastating, and socially debilitating.

We must also take into consideration the impact that the current pandemic, social unrest, and remote learning is having on the mental health and well-being of teachers, administrators, and parents. This makes the implementation of SEL competencies and skills into the very fabric of school-related structures, practices, and family dynamics a high priority. This focus on SEL should not be considered as an add-on, an additional responsibility, a burden, and distraction to teaching the core content. Instead, it is exactly what is needed in this time of extreme uncertainty, insecurity, unpredictability, and inequity. SEL is definitely not a panacea but an effort to prevent further delay and exclusion of LTELs from fulfilling their hopes and dreams for a brighter future.

Connecting and integrating the concepts of SEL, positive beliefs about children and their families, innovative instructional practices of teaching core content and hands-on, collaborative, and inclusive leadership skills of school and district administrators is essential to addressing the current challenges we face to prepare children to be better equipped to thrive in an evolving global community. In prior chapters every attempt was made to address the following five essential questions:

Why?	Why we need to change our school structures, instructional practices, relationships with colleagues, our own thinking, and family connections.
What?	The rationale and a long body of research on SEL, academic language, reading comprehension, and writing for ELs and LTELs.
How?	Three chapters devoted to how "old" and "new" research and practices show us how to explicitly teach language, literacy, and SEL integrated within any content area.
Where?	We provided ideas for teaching the language, literacy, and SEL strategies in remote and in class lessons.
When?	The notion that we need to teach academic language, vocabulary as necessary from texts students are to read, and reading comprehension and writing strategies in all classrooms, every day, by all teachers. LTEL need explicit instruction and their application while reading, discussing, and writing at least 3,000—5,000 words per year. SEL competencies undergird the intensive learning.

As we have seen in many sites, the integration of SEL with all instructional approaches becomes the school's goal and everyone's effort through a comprehensive professional development program (Zacarian, Calderón and Gottlieb 2021). It is not just the job of ESL teachers to teach English as a second language anymore. It is not just the role of a reading specialist to enhance the reading skills of LTEL. In order for LTEL to do well in all subject areas, all subject area teachers now can be part of the LTEL success by learning and practicing the strategies we describe here that have already been proven to be effective. Co-teaching by ESL and core content teachers needs to be aligned and made more effective through extensive professional development that includes all the components listed here.

TLCs' Support Sequence, Structures, Strategies, Sharing, and Success

TLCs are Teachers Learning Communities where teachers in small teams work during the day to study their implementation of new information and instructional strategies (Calderón 1999, 2018 Zacarian, Calderón, and Gottlieb 2021). These are places and spaces for collaboration that are set aside to solve implementation problems, develop lessons, model effective strategies for one another, celebrate their and their students' successes, and plan agendas for the next TLC. They can be anywhere from 35 to 60 minutes. These are different from brief professional development workshops or other school committees or learning communities. These are focused solely on LTEL instruction. These *structures* are respected and supported by the administration without interruptions. They are *sequential* in nature because they build on the participants' learning. Teachers take turns *sharing* effective techniques or modeling a new way of approaching a *strategy* with better *success*.

What often hampers the implementation process of effective practices and the consistency and focus of Teachers Learning Communities (TLCs) is when professional development is nothing more than a series of disjointed workshops on disconnected topics that many times contradict one another. Instead, effective schools for ELs are those that adopt a model that integrates language, literacy and SEL into each subject area. Moreover, when all teachers learn the same sequence, structures, and strategies, and share through TLCs, peer coaching, and joint lesson planning, all students accelerate their learning. When students see the depth of collaboration between teachers, they adapt their collaboration as a model for peer learning. Teachers are most effective when they model the positive peer interaction and peer collaboration that are needed in the classroom for all the partner and team-based activities.

The diagram below illustrates the significant impact of in-depth support in order to ensure fidelity of implementation, quality control, sustainability, and capacity building at multiple levels of the organization. Where professional development is provided without any form of support or messaging from the leadership team that this is important, the initiative is short lived and usually followed by the typical refrain that "we tried it and it didn't work." The value of TLCs has more to do with leveraging of the talents, knowledge, and experience of the teachers to further motivate, inspire, and guide the team to be more collaborative and cooperative in putting the needs of the students first. This practice will not only sustain any new initiative but will create a school climate and culture that is better aligned vertically and horizontally and is more consistent in its messaging and practices. When this foundational work is a common practice, teachers and administrators will be better able to identify conditions that create LTELs and will be better equipped to disrupt existing systemic deficiencies that may have contributed to the problem.

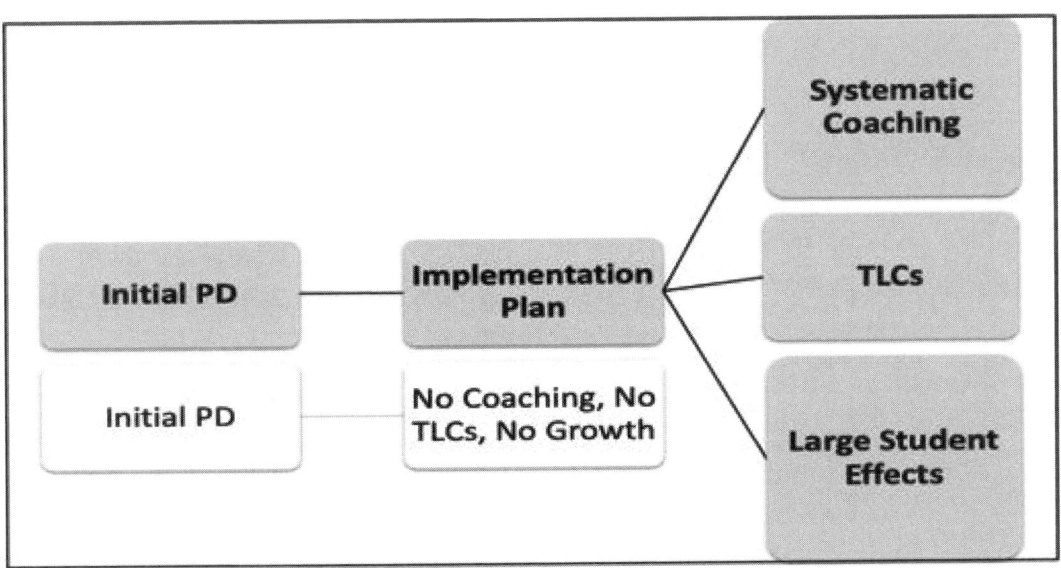

Figure 7.1 Expected outcomes with and without a follow-up teacher support system

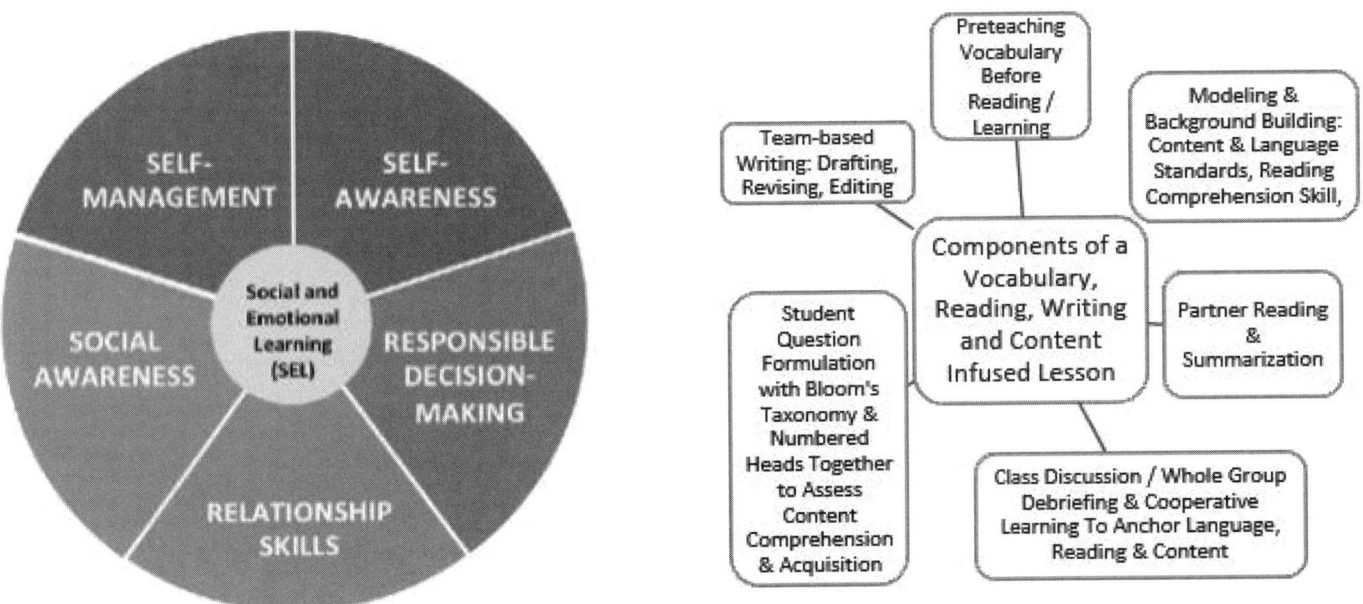

Figure 7.2 SEL and ExC-ELL™ components

Another way of looking at the integration is with a sequential list of all components, as shown in Table 7.1. Together, they form the framework for a comprehensive instruction in all subjects by all teachers. As we further explore the 12 Components of ExC-ELLTM, it will become increasingly apparent that SEL competencies are embedded in each and every one of the components. It then becomes the role of the teacher to point out, identify, accentuate, and reinforce the SEL competencies "explicitly" so that the deeper learning behind the activity is clearly understood.

FIVE CORE SEL COMPETENCIES	ExC-ELL 12 COMPONENTS
Self-Awareness • labeling one's feelings • relating feelings and thoughts to behavior • accurate self-assessment of strengths and challenges • self-efficacy • optimism **Self-Management** • regulating one's emotions • managing stress • self-control • self-motivation • setting and achieving goals **Social Awareness** • perspective taking • empathy • respecting diversity • understanding social and ethical norms of behavior • recognizing family, school, and community supports **Relationship Skills** • building relationships with diverse individuals and groups • communicating clearly • working cooperatively • resolving conflicts • seeking help **Responsible Decision-Making** • considering the well-being of self and others • recognizing one's responsibility to behave ethically • basing decisions on safety, social, and ethical considerations • evaluating realistic consequences of various actions • making constructive, safe choices for self, relationships, and school	1. Preteaching of vocabulary 2. Teacher Think-Alouds 3. Student Peer Reading 4. Peer Summaries 5. Depth of Word Studies/Grammar 6. Class debriefings/discussions 7. Cooperative learning activities 8. Formulating Questions and Numbered Heads 9. Round Table Reviews 10. Pre-writing and drafting 11. Revising/Editing 12. Reading final product

Table 7.1 How SEL and ExC-ELL™ work together

In Essence . . .

Intentionally and explicitly teaching specific SEL competencies to be practiced during Partner Reading, vocabulary practice, or writing in teams will no longer leave the evolution of those skills to chance. SEL practices such as morning meetings and community circles where shared agreements, norms of collaboration, and learning protocols such as accountable talk are discussed, practiced, and agreed to, should be posted in visible places such as on table tents or on anchor charts. This would have the effect of reinforcing the students' desire and ability to call on those skills in practice. Instead of English-dominant students being resentful and impatient when partnering with an EL or an LTEL, they are more adept and prepared to practice specific SEL competencies that have been discussed collaboratively and agreed to collectively. This ensures that equitable practices of inclusion, appreciation, differentiation, and learning in a safe learning environment help LTELs dispel the long-term effects and trauma of past experiences of embarrassment, shaming, and fear.

Once these fundamental agreements and practices are understood and embedded in the expectations of a class climate and culture, they become the norm of "who we are." Beginning with "baby steps" is most suitable when introducing any new skill or competency. Teachers need time to experiment with the integration of SEL with core content, make mistakes, and reflect on those valuable experiences in their TLCs. Once this new normal becomes the norm, then all students will be better prepared to perform more complex tasks, understand more complex texts, and accelerate their learning and progress toward becoming college and career ready.

Conclusion

An integrated approach to the professional development and implementation of SEL, language, literacy, and content for LTEL means that an integrated view of teaching and learning, such as the one in Figure 7.2, is deeply embedded into the mindset and practice of teachers and supported by administrators. This illustration shows the compatibility of the two components and better illustrates the inherent connectivity in a more explicit and transparent way. For example, a simple practice such as Partner Reading and Summarization, when done properly, has the potential to motivate and accelerate the desire and capacity of LTELs to increase their reading skills exponentially. As we often see with Partner Reading as a secondary outcome that is not "explicitly" built into the practice, there is the gradual evolution of the participating students' ability to develop friendships, bond, and strengthen specific SEL skills such as empathy, compassion, patience, and social awareness. This is especially notable when stronger English speakers are paired with EL/LTEL.

Personal Reflections and Collegial Discussions

1. Where do we go from here? What do we need to address first?

   _____

   _____

   _____

2. What outcomes do we expect?

   _____

   _____

   _____

3. What kind of grid do we use for the what, why, how, who does, and when?

   _____

   _____

   _____

4. What measures do we collect for each task?

   _____

   _____

   _____

5. What benchmarks, criteria indicators do we establish in order to gauge our progress and where to dive back?

   _____

   _____

   _____

 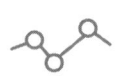 

References

Adams, J. M. *Social and Emotional Learning Gaining New Focus under Common Core.* EdSource, 2013.

Allen, M. "Planning for Better Professional Development in an Uncertain Future." 2020. August 6 https://www.edutopia.org/article/planning-better-professional-development-uncertain-future

Anchorage School District. PreK–Adult Social and Emotional Learning Standards. SEL Steering Committee. 2004.

August, D., I. L. Beck, M. Calderón, D. J. Francis, N. K. Lesaux, and T. Shanahan. "Instruction and Professional Development." In *Developing Reading and Writing in Second Language Learners. Lessons from the Report of the National Literacy Panel on Language-Minority Children and Youth*, edited by D. August and T. Shanahan. New York, NY: Routledge, 2008.

August, D., and T. Shanahan, eds. *Developing Reading and Writing in Second-language Learners: Lessons from the Report of the National Literacy Panel on Language-Minority Children and Youth.* New York, NY: Routledge, 2008.

Beck, I. L., M. G. McKeown, and L. Kucan. *Bringing Words to Life. Robust Vocabulary Instruction.* New York, NY: The Guilford Press, 2002.

Beck, I. L., M. G. McKeown, and L. Kucan. "Choosing Words to Teach." In *Teaching and Learning Vocabulary: Bringing Research to Practice*, edited by A. Hiebert and M. Kamil, 207–222. Nahwah, NJ: Lawrence Erlbaum Associates, 2005.

Beck, I. L., C. A. Perfetti, and M. G. McKeown "The Effects of Long-term Vocabulary Instruction on Lexical Access and Reading Comprehension." *Journal of Educational Psychology* 74 (1982): 506–21.

Beyond Differences. "No One Eats Alone." 2021. http://www.nooneeatsalone.org/welcome/

Brackett, M. Permission to Feel. Yale Center for Emotional Intelligence. New York, NY: Celadon Books, 2019.

Calderón, M. Teachers Learning Communities for cooperation in diverse settings. In M. Calderón & R.E. Slavin (Eds.). *Building community through cooperative learning. Special issue of Theory into Practice Journal.* Spring, 38 (2). Columbus, OH: Ohio State University, 1999.

Calderón, M. (2009). "Language, Literacy and Knowledge for ELLs." In *Better: Evidence-Based Education*, Vol. 1, edited by R. Slavin, 14–15. Heslington, England: University of York, 2011.

Calderón, M., ed. *Breaking through: Effective Instruction and Assessment for Reaching English Learners.* Bloomington, IN: Solution Tree Press, 2012.

Calderón, M. E. *RIGOR! Reading Instructional Goals for Older Readers: Reading Program for 6th—12th Students with Interrupted Formal Education. English and Spanish Versions.* New York, NY: Benchmark Education Co., 2007a.

Calderón, M. E. *Teaching Reading to English Language Learners, Grades 6-12: A Framework for Improving Achievement in the Content Areas.* Thousand Oaks, CA: Corwin Press, 2007b

Calderón, M. E. *Coaching Teachers with ELs: ExC-ELL Manual*. Washington, DC: MC & Associates, 2010.

Calderón, M. E. "Teaching Writing to English Language Learners." In *Teaching Writing to ELs in Secondary Schools.* In Better: Evidence-based Education. Heslington, England: University of York, 2011.

Calderón, M.E. *Coaching teachers with English Learners: ExC-ELL Manual* for administrators and coaches. Washington, DC: Margarita Calderón & Associates. 2017

Calderón, M. E. *Expediting Comprehension for English Language Learners (ExC-ELL) Foundations Manual.* Washington, DC: Margarita Calderón & Associate, 2018

Calderón, M. E. *Expediting Comprehension for English Language Learners (ExC-ELL) Foundations Manual.* Washington, DC: Margarita Calderón & Associates, 2020.

Calderón, M., August, D., R. Slavin, A. Cheung, D. Durán & N. Madden (2005). Bringing words to life in classrooms with English language learners. In Hiebert, A & M. Kamil (eds.) *Teaching and Learning Vocabulary: Bringing research to practice* (pp. 115 – 136). Nahwah, NJ: Lawrence Erlbaum Associates.

Calderón, M., Carreón, A., Cantú, J., & Minaya-Rowe, L. Expediting comprehension for English language learners: Participants' manual. New York: Benchmark Education, 2010.

Calderón, M. E., G. Espino, and S. Slakk. *Integrando lenguaje, lectura, escritura y contenidos en español e inglés. Integrating Language, Reading, Writing and Content in English and in Spanish*. Los Angeles, CA: Velazquez Press, 2019.

Calderón, M. E., R. Hertz-Lazarowitz, and R. E. Slavin. "Effects of Bilingual Cooperative Integrated Reading and Composition on Students Making the Transition from Spanish to English Reading." *The Elementary School Journal* 99, no. 2 (November 1998).

http://www.journals.uchicago.edu/doi/abs/10.1086/461920. In the What Works Clearinghouse: https://ies.ed.gov/ncee/wwc/EvidenceSnapshot/47

Calderón, M. E., and L. Minaya-Rowe. *Preventing Long-term ELs: Transforming Schools to Meet Core Standards.* Thousand Oaks, CA: Corwin Press, 2011.

Calderón, M. E., and L. Minaya-Rowe. *Designing and Implementing Two-way Bilingual Programs: A Step-by-Step Guide for Administrators, Teachers, and Parents.* Thousand Oaks, CA: Corwin Press, 2003.

Calderón, M. E., S. Slakk, and H. Montenegro. Promises Fulfilled: *A Learner's Guide for Supporting English Learners.* Bloomington, IN: Solution Tree Press, 2017.

Calderón, M. E., and S. Slakk. *Success with Multicultural Newcomers & English Learners: Proven Practices for School Leadership Teams.* Alexandria, VA: Association for Supervision and Curriculum Development, 2019.

Calderón, M. (1999). Teachers Learning Communities for cooperation in diverse settings. In M. Calderón & R.E. Slavin (Eds.). Building community through cooperative learning. Special issue of Theory into Practice Journal. Spring, 38 (2). Columbus, OH: Ohio State UniversityCalderón, M. E., M. Trejo, and H. Montenegro. *Literacy Strategies for English Learners in Core Content Secondary Classrooms.* Bloomington, IN: Solution Tree Press, 2016.

Calderón, M., ed. *Breaking through: Effective Instruction and Assessment for Reaching English Learners.* Bloomington, IN: Solution Tree Press, 2012.Calderón, M. E. RIGOR! *Reading Instructional Goals for Older Readers: Reading Program for 6th—12th Students with Interrupted Formal Education. English and Spanish Versions.* New York, NY: Benchmark Education Co., 2007a.

Calderón, M. E. *Teaching Reading to English Language Learners, Grades 6-12: A Framework for Improving Achievement in the Content Areas.* Thousand Oaks, CA: Corwin Press, 2007b.

Calderón, M. E., Carreón, A., Slakk, S. & J. Peyton. *Expediting Comprehension for English Language Learners (ExC-ELL) Foundations Manual.* Washington, DC: Margarita Calderón & Associates, 2017.

Calderón, M.E. & L. Tartaglia. Core-content teachers: You can provide good distance learning for English Learners. *ASCD, Educational Leadership Exclusive,* May 13. Alexandria, VA: ASCD. 2020.

Carlo, M. S., D. August, and C. E. Snow. "Sustained Vocabulary-learning Strategy Instruction for English Language Learners." In *Teaching and Learning Vocabulary: Bringing Research to Practice,* edited by E. H. Hiebert, and M. L. Kamil, 137–54. Mahwah, NJ: Lawrence Erlbaum, 2005.

CASEL. *The CASEL Guide to Schoolwide Social and Emotional Learning. Collaborative for Academic, Social, and Emotional Learning.* Chicago. 2019a. https://schoolguide.casel.org

CASEL. *Collaborating States Initiative Resources (CSI). Collaborative for Academic, Social, and Emotional Learning.* Chicago. 2019b. https://casel.org/csi-resources/

CASEL. *Core SEL Competencies. Collaborative for Academic, Social, and Emotional Learning.* Chicago. 2019c. https://casel.org/core-competencies/

CASEL. *SEL 3 Signature Practices Playbook.* Chicago 2019. https://casel.org/sel-3-signature-practices/

Center for Reaching and Teaching the Whole Child. *Culturally Responsive Teaching (CRT).* 2015. http://crtwc.org

Chall, J. S. "American Reading Achievement: Should We Worry?" *Research in the Teaching of English* 30 (1996): 303–10.

Common Core State Standards. *English Language Arts & Literacy in History/Social Studies, Science, and Technical Subjects.* 2010. http://www.corestandards.org/assets/CCSSI_ELA%20Standards.pdf

Crowley, B., and B. Saide. "Building Empathy in Classrooms and Schools." *Education Week.* January 20, 2016. http://www.edweek.org/tm/articles/2016/01/20/building-empathy-in-classrooms-and-schools.html

Cunningham, A. E., and K. E. Stanovich. "What Reading Does for the Mind." *American Educator* (Spring–Summer, 1998): 8–17. v22 n1-2 p8-15 Spr-Sum

DePaoli, J., M. Atwell, J. Bridgeland, and T. Shriver. Respected: Perspectives of Youth on High School and *Social and Emotional Learning*. Report prepared for CASEL. Washington: Civic Enterprises with Peter D. Hart Research Associates, 2018.

Dickenson, P. "Reform for English Language Learners." Education Week. January 12, 2012. http://blogs.edweek.org/edweek/rick_hess_straight_up/2012/01/reform_for_english_language_learn-ers.html#

Durlak, J. A., R. P. Weissberg, A. B. Dymnicki, R. D. Taylor, and K. B. Schellinger. "The Impact of Enhancing Students' Social and Emotional Learning: A Meta-analysis of School-based Universal Interventions." *Child Development* 82, no. 1: 405–32, 2011.

Dweck, C. S. Self-theories: *Their Role in Motivation, Personality, and Development.* New York, NY: Taylor & Francis, 2000.

Dweck, C. S. Mindset: *The New Psychology of Success*. New York, NY: Ballantine Books, 2016.

Elias, M. J., and H. Arnold, eds. *The Educator's Guide to Emotional Intelligence and Academic Achievement: Social-emotional Learning in the Classroom*. Thousand Oaks, CA: Corwin Press, 2006.

El Paso ISD. *Social and Emotional Learning Standards.* https://www.episd.org/Page/7129, 2017.

Elias, M. J., J. E. Zins, R. P. Weissberg, K. S. Frey, M. T. Greenberg, N. M. Haynes, et al. *Promoting Social and Emotional Learning: Guidelines for Educators*. Alexandria, VA: Association for Supervision and Curriculum Development, 1997.

Eunice Kennedy Shriver National Institute of Child Health and Human Development, NIH, DHHS. (2000). Report of the National Reading Panel: Teaching Children to Read: Reports of the Subgroups (00-4754). Washington, DC: U.S. Government Printing Office

Fisher, D., and Frey, N. "Show & Tell: A Video Column / Three Conditions English Learners Need to Thrive." In *Building Bridges for ELLs*. Alexandria, VA: Association for Supervision and Curriculum Development. December 2019/January 2020. Vol. 77, no. 4. http://www.ascd.org/publications/educational-leadership/dec19/vol77/num04/Three-Conditions-English-Learners-Need-to-Thrive.aspx

Fisher, D., Frey, N., and Smith, D. All Learning Is Social and Emotional: *Helping Students Develop Essential Skills for the Classroom and Beyond*. Alexandria, VA: Association for Supervision and Curriculum Development, 2019.

Flannery, M. E. The Epidemic of Anxiety among Today's Students. Washington, DC: neaTODAY, 2019. http://neatoday.org/2018/03/28/the-epidemic-of-student-anxiety/

Forum. *Forum for Educators: An inclusive community to uplift every single soul*. December 2019. https://www.millenniumforum.org/

Gándara, P. and Zárate, M. E. "Can the LCFF Improve Teaching and Learning for EL Students? A Review of the Emerging Research in California and Directions for Future Implementation." *Peabody Journal of Education* 94, no. 2 (2019).

Goleman, D. *Emotional Intelligence*. New York, NY: Bantam, 1995.

Gottlieb, M. (2016). Assessing English language learners: Bridges to educational equity: Connecting academic language proficiency to student achievement (2nd ed.). Thousand Oaks, CA: Corwin.

Graham, S., Harris, K. and M. Hebert. Informing writing: The benefits of formative assessment. New York: The Carnegie Corporation of New York. 2011

Graham, S. and Hebert, M. Writing to read: Evidence for how writing can improve reading. New York: The Carnegie Corporation of New York. 2010.

Graham, S., and Perin, D. *Writing Next: Effective Strategies to Improve Writing of Adolescents in Middle and High Schools.* New York, NY: Carnegie Corporation of New York, 2007.

Graves, M., August, D., and Carlo, M. "Teaching 50,000 Words." *Better: Evidence-based Education* 3, no. 2 (Winter, 2011): 6–7. Baltimore, MD: Johns Hopkins University.

Great Kindness Challenge. https://thegreatkindnesschallenge.com. 2021

Gregoire, C. "5 Surprising Ways Mindfulness Can Change You." *Huffington Post.* March 5, 2015. http://www.huffingtonpost.com/2015/03/05/surprising-mindfulness-be_n_6771374.html

Hakuta, K. Kenji Hakuta on ELLs and the Common Core State Standards: Video. Palo Alto, CA: SCOPE Center. https://edpolicy.stanford.edu/library/video/485

Hansell, S., and R. Slavin, *Cooperative Learning and Interracial Friendships.* Paper presented at the Annual Convention of the American Psychological Association, New York, 1979.

Hart, B., and T. R. Risley, *Meaningful Differences in the Everyday Experience of Young American Children.* Baltimore, MD: Paul H. Brookes Publishing Company, 1995.

Illinois State Board of Education. *Social/Emotional Learning Standards.* Illinois Learning Standards. 2019. https://www.isbe.net/Pages/Social-Emotional-Learning-Standards.aspx

Jagers, R. J., D. Rivas-Drake, and T. Borowski, T. *Equity & Social and Emotional Learning: A Cultural Analysis.* CASEL. *Measuring SEL Using Data to Inspire Practice.* 2018. https://measuringsel.casel.org/wp-content/uploads/2018/11/Frameworks-Equity.pdf

Johnson, D., R. Johnson, and E. Johnson Holubec. *The Nuts & Bolts of Cooperative Learning.* Edina, MN: Interaction Book Co., 2006.

Kazakoff E. & Mitchell A. "Cultivating a growth mindset with educational technology", Lexia. from: www.lexialearning.com. 2017.

Kennedy, M. J. and Deshler, D. D. Literacy Instruction, Technology, and Students with Learning Disabilities: Research We Have, Research We Need. In *Learning Disability Journal,* Volume: 33 issue: 4, page(s): 289-298 November 1, 2010.

Kohli, R and Solórzano, D. "Teachers Please Learn Our Names!" Published online: 23 May 2012. https://www.tandfonline.com/doi/abs/10.1080/13613324.2012.674026

Lantieri, L. *Mindfulness Practice during a CASEL Webinar for the School Guide for Systemic SEL Implementation.* Chicago, IL: Author, 2015.

Lantieri, L., and Nambiar, M. "Cultivating the Social, Emotional, and Inner Lives of Children and Teachers." *Reclaiming Children and Youth Journal* 21, no. 2 (Summer, 2012). www.reclaimingjournal.com

Lazarín, M. *COVID-19 Spotlights the Inequities Facing English Learner Students, as Nonprofit Organizations Seek to Mitigate Challenges.* Washington, DC: The Migration Policy Institute, June 2020. https://www.migrationpolicy.org/news/covid-19-inequities-english-learner-students

Markowitz, N. In Adams, J. M. (2013). Social and emotional learning gaining new focus under Common Core. EdSource.

Menasce Horowitz, J., and Graf, N. *Most U.S. Teens See Anxiety and Depression as a Major Problem Among Their Peers.* Washington, DC: Pew Research Center, 2019. https://www.pewsocialtrends.org/2019/02/20/most-u-s-teens-see-anxiety-and-depression-as-a-major-problem-among-their-peers/

Merrow, C. *Journaling as a Social and emotional learning Practice.* Empowering Education. 2019. https://empoweringeducation.org/journaling-as-a-social-emotional-practice/

Moats, L. *Teaching Reading is Rocket Science, 2020.* Washington, DC: American Federation of Teachers, 2020.

Montenegro, H. "Classroom and School Structures for Student and Teacher Support Systems." In *Literacy Strategies for English Learners in Core Content Secondary Classrooms*, edited by M. E. Calderón, M. Trejo, and H. Montenegro. Bloomington, IN: Solution Tree Press, 2016.

Nagy, W. "Why Vocabulary Instruction Needs to be Long-term and Comprehensive." In *Teaching and Learning Vocabulary: Bringing Research to Practice*, edited by E. H. Hiebert and M. L. Kamil, 27–44. Mahwah, NJ: Lawrence Erlbaum, 2005.

Nagy, W. "Metalinguistic Awareness and the Vocabulary Comprehension Connection." In *Vocabulary Acquisition: Implications for Reading Comprehension*, edited by R. K. Wagner, A. E. Muse, and K. R. Tannenbaum, 52–77. New York: Guilford Press, 2007.

Nation, I. S. P. (2009). *Teaching ESL/EFL Reading and Writing.* New York: Routledge.

National Academies of Sciences, Engineering, and Medicine. *The Integration of Immigrants into American Society*. The National Academies Press. 2017. http://real.mtak.hu/88788/1/401-1-1278-1-10-20170930.pdf

National Commission on Social, Emotional, and Academic Development. *From a Nation at Risk to a Nation at Hope*. Aspen Institute, 2018a.

National Commission on Social, Emotional, and Academic Development. *The Practice Base for How We Learn: Supporting Students' Social, Emotional, and Academic Development*. Aspen Institute. 2018b. https://www.aspeninstitute.org/publications/practice-base-learn-supporting-students-social-emotion-al-academic-development/

National Council of Teachers of English. *Writing Now: A Policy Brief.* Author, 2008. https://secure.ncte.org/library/NCTEFiles/Resources/PolicyResearch/WrtgResearchBrief.pdf

National Reading Panel. *Teaching Children to Read: An Evidence-based Assessment of the Scientific Research Literature on Reading and its Implications for Reading Instruction.* Rockville, MD: National Institute of Child Health and Human Development, 2000.

NGSS (Next Generation Science Standards). *Next Generation Science Standards for Public Schools.* 2019. https://www.nextgenscience.org/get-to-know

Oakland USD. *Pre-K-Adult Social and Emotional Learning Standards.* 2018. https://drive.google.com/file/d/0B2DcKbJpERRRQmYzV0NqQUU3MFQ0SnVGbzlWNmhldUxENE5R/view

Olsen, L. *Reparable Harm: Fulfilling the Unkept Promise of Educational Opportunity for Long Term English Learners.* Californians Together. 2010. www.californianstogether.org

Pearson, P.; Moje, E.; and Greenleaf, C. "Literacy and Science: Each in the Service of the Other." *Science* (2010): Science 23 Apr 2010: Vol. 328, Issue 5977, pp. 459-463 .

Pennebaker, J. W. Homepage. 2019. http://homepage.psy.utexas.edu/homepage/faculty/pennebaker/Home2000/JWPhome.html

Pennebaker, J. W. *Writing to Heal: A Guided Journal for Recovering from Trauma and Emotional Upheaval.* Oakland, CA: New Harbinger Publications. 2004.

Ricks Resources. *Acts of Kindness Task Cards.* Teacher Synergy. 2016. Inc. https://www.teacherspayteachers.com/Product/Kindness-Task-Cards-48-Social-Skills-738305

SCCOE. *My Name, My Identity.* Santa Clara County Office of Education. Santa Clara, CA. 2021. https://www.mynamemyidentity.org

Sapon-Shevin, M. Because We Can Change the World: *A Practical Guide to Building Cooperative, Inclusive Classroom Communities.* Boston, MA: Allyn & Bacon, 2010.

Schaps, E., V. Battistich, and D. Solomon. "Community in School as Key to Student Growth: Findings from the Child Development Project." In *Building Academic Success on Social and Emotional Learning: What Does the Research Say?* edited by J. E. Zins, R. P. Weissberg, M. C. Wang, and H. J. Walberg. New York, NY: Teachers College Press, 2004.

Senechal, M., and E. H. Cornell. "Vocabulary Acquisition through Shared Reading." *Reading Research Quarterly* 28, no. 4 (October–November–December 1993): 360–74.

Shanahan, T. "The Six Goals of an Ideal Vocabulary Lesson." Shanahan blog. June 13, 2020. https://shanahanonliteracy.com/blog/the-six-goals-of-an-ideal-vocabulary-curriculum

Slavin, R. E. "Cooperative Learning." *Review of Educational Research.* American Educational Research Association. June 1980. https://doi.org/10.3102/00346543050002315

Slavin, R. E. and M. Calderón, eds. *Effective Programs for Latino Students.* Nahwah, NJ: Lawrence Erlbaum, 2001.

Slavin, R. E., C. Lake, A. Inns, A. Baye, D. Dachet, and J. Haslam. *A Quantitative Synthesis of Research on Writing Approaches in Grades 2 to 12.* Best Evidence Encyclopedia (BEE). Baltimore, MD: Center for Research and Reform in Education, 2019.

Slavin R. E. and N. A. Madden. *One million children: SUCCESS FOR ALL.* Thousand Oaks: CA: Corwin Press 2001.

Smith, D., D. Fisher, and N. Frey. *Better than Carrots or Sticks: Restorative Practices for Positive Classroom Management.* Alexandria, VA: Association for Supervision and Curriculum Development, 2015.

Srinivasan, M. SEL Every Day: *Integration Social and Emotional Learning with Instruction in Secondary Classrooms.* New York, NY: Norton Books in Education, 2019.

Stahl, S. A. "Four Problems with Teaching Word Meanings: And What to Do to Make Vocabulary and Integral Part of Instruction." In *Teaching and Learning Vocabulary: Bringing Research to Practice*, edited by E. H. Hiebert and M. L. Kamil, 95–114. Mahwah, NJ: Lawrence Erlbaum Associates, Inc., 2005.

TESOL. *The Six Principles for Exemplary Teaching of English Learners. Teaching English to Speakers of Other Languages*. TESOL International Association. Annapolis Junction, MD: TESCOL Press, 2019.

USDOE. *Learning remotely in the age of COVID-19: Lessons from evidence and concerns for equity*. Regional Educational Laboratory, US Department of Education. 2021. https://ies.ed.gov/ncee/edlabs/regions/midatlantic/app/Docs/Events/Remote_Learning_Webinar_Slides_508.pdf

Wang, M. C., and H. J. Walberg, eds. *Building Academic Success on Social and Emotional Learning: What Does the Research Say?* New York, NY: Teachers College Press.

Vietnamese American Young Leaders Association of New Orleans (VAYLA). Adapted from *ESL: Lost in the System*. New Orleans, LA: VAYLA, 2012.

Zacarian, D., M. E. Calderón, and M. Gottlieb. *Beyond Crises: Overcoming Linguistic and Cultural Inequities in Communities, Schools, and Classrooms.* Thousand Oaks, CA: CORWIN, 2021.

Zins, J. E., R. P. Weissberg, M. C. Wang, and H. J. Walberg, eds. *Building Academic Success on Social and Emotional Learning: What Does the Research Say?* New York, NY: Teachers College Press, 2004.